BACTERIAL BIOREMEDIATION OF HEAVY METALS IN TANNERY EFFLUENT

Editor

Dr. Hanan Selman Hessan
College of Dentistry, University of Babylon, Babylon Province, Iraq

Published by

JPS Scientific Publications
India

Published by

JPS Scientific Publications, Tamil Nadu, India.
E.mail: jpsscientificpublications@gmail.com
Website: www.jpsscientificpublications.com

Published in India.

International Standard Book Number (ISBN): 978-93-91342-09-8

JPS Scientific Publications also publishes its books in a variety of Electronic formats. Some content that appears in print may not be available in Electronic formats. For more information visit our publication website www.jpsscientificpublications.com

ABSTRACT

The tannery effluent was collected from the Vellore district of Tamil Nadu, India and bioremediated. Physico – chemical characteristics of the collected tannery effluent was analyzed. The tannery effluent was acidic nature with brown colour and emitted unpleasant smell. High value of TSS and TDS and BOD and COD, calcium, magnesium, sodium, potassium, fluoride, nitrate, nitrite, sulphate and the toxic heavy metals chromium, nickel, zinc, copper and iron were recorded in the collected tannery effluent sample. Ten different bacterial isolates *viz.*, *Pseudomonas* sp. (P1), *Proteus* sp., *Bacillus* sp., *Escherichia* sp., *Serratia* sp., *Pseudomonas* sp. (P2), *Staphylococcus* sp., *Enterobacter* sp., *Alcaligenes* sp., *Micrococcus* sp. and *Staphylococcus* sp. were identified. The bacterial isolates were screened for its resistance against toxic heavy metals. All the ten isolate were resistant to all the heavy metals. Heavy metal adsorption by living bacterial cells (Bioaccumulation), dead bacterial cells (Biosorption) and immobilized bacterial cells (Immobilization) was studied. Immobilized (Sodium alginate) bacterial cells were considered as the best was for the bioremediation of heavy metals. The bacterial isolates which were identified in genus level were subjected to 16S rRNA sequencing and identified in species level. The bacteria *Bacillus* sp. confirmed as was confirmed as *Bacillus subtilis*, *Serratia* sp. was confirmed as *Serratia marcescens* and *Pseudomonas* sp. was confirmed as *Pseudomonas fluorescens*. The bacterial isolate *Bacillus subtilis*, *Serratia marcescens, Pseudomonas fluorescens* were selected for optimization study based on heavy metal adsorption. The collected tannery effluent was inoculated with (immobilized beads) 5 per cent inoculum containing $>10^5$ cfu/ml of bacterial consortium (*Bacillus subtilis* + *Serratia marcescens* + *Pseudomonas fluorescens*), and air was passed continuously using an aerator. After 6 months, the sample was filtered under aseptic condition and physico - chemical parameters were estimated. The colour of the bioremediated tannery effluent sample was black to colourless and odorless. The physico – chemical characteristics of the bioremediated tannery effluent was significantly reduced after 6 months.

Key words: Tannery effluent, Heavy metals, Bacteria, Bioremediation and Immobilized beads.

Contents

1. INTRODUCTION

Environmental pollution has become a major concern of developing countries in the last few decades. There is a growing sense of global urgency regarding the pollution of our environment by an array of chemicals used in various activities (Palaniappan *et al.*, 2009). Pollution has become a serious threat and has brought drastic changes and ill-effects to the growing population as well as the mother Earth. Pollution of environment is a major global problem due to the rapid urbanization and industrialization has led to increased disposal of pollutants such as heavy metals, radio nuclides and various types of organics and inorganics pollutants into the environment. Water and soil pollution by heavy metals is an emerging problem in urbo industrialized countries. Since, the advent of development through mining and smelting, tanning, sewage, warfare and metallurgical industries the survival of plants and animals are much affected (Xi *et al.*, 2009).

Industrial pollution has been continues to be a major factor causing the degradation of the environment around us, affecting the water we use, the air we breathe and the soil we live on. Of these, the pollution of water is arguably the most serious threat to current human welfare. India is an agriculture based country and a major user of water resource for irrigation but, there is a great demand in water resource for irrigation (Singh *et al.*, 2005). The water for irrigation while contains gallons and gallons of effluents are let out into water sources as untreated. The most important effluent discharging industries are tannery industries, sugar mills, thermal power plants, paper mills, textiles, distilleries, fertilizer units, electroplating plants, sago industries, oil refineries, pesticide and herbicide industries. These industrial effluents containing heavy metals pose a serious threat to the ecosystem (Amathussalam *et al.*, 2002). Use of these industrial effluents and sewage sludge for agriculture have become a common practice in India as a result of which the toxic metals get transferred and accumulated into plant tissue from soil (Mahavi, 2005). The disposal of sewage water is a major problem of big cities worldwide. Several toxic elements accumulate in soils as a consequence of industrial and urban activities and because of the use of untreated sewage sludge (Mehdi *et al.*, 2003).

Among the several industries, tannery industry is one of the oldest cottage industries in India which has taken a predominant place in the country's economy. It discharges many toxic pollutants like chromium, sulphides, phenolic compounds, magnesium, sodium, potassium, dyes and solvents. Improper disposal of such hazardous tannery effluents is an acute problem to the environment. Tannery wastes are ranked as the highest pollutants among all the industrial wastes (Soyaslan and Karaguzel, 2007). In agricultural system, the toxic pollutants reduces light penetration and photosynthesis and also some of toxic elements are mutagenic, carcinogenic and allergenic (Aksu and Cagatay, 2006; Kumar *et al.*, 2006).

A variety of chemicals are used in the tanning industries, including lime, sodium chloride, sodium carbonate, ammonium chloride, sulphuric acid, tannins and dyes. The discharged effluents from the processing units are stored in large lagoons and the dissolved salts percolated into the surrounding soil. The waste water discharged for 100 kg of skins and hides and skins processed, varies from 3000 litres to 3200 litres. The largest polluting material in the tanning industry is common salt. For every 10 tons of salted hides and skins processed 2-3 tons of salt is removed and in addition another one ton of salt was removed. (Altaf *et al.*, 2008).

Tamil Nadu is the state having much share in the industrial economy of India. The tannery industry as a major sharecropper of the foreign exchange earner has in the recent past become a highly controversial subject because of the scope with which it is viewed in the midst of environmentalists. Vellore District is one of the important Districts of Tamil Nadu where, more than 1,000 tanneries both of large and small scale are concentrated (Lavanya and Venkata Krishnan, 1997).

According to the World Health Organization (WHO, 2005), the metals of the most immediate concern are cadmium, chromium, cobalt, copper, lead, nickel, mercury and zinc. The presence of such metals (>5 g cm^3) in aquatic environments, cause severe damage to aquatic life and killing of microorganisms during a biological water purification process. Moreover, these metals have been exacting consequences on humans such as brain damage, reproductive system failures, nervous system failures, tumour formation, etc., (Mahavi, 2005).

The Tannery industry releases waste water is a serious consequence from the pollution point of view for streams, freshwater and land used for agriculture. The lack of awareness in the modern industrial practice has resulted in the discharge of tannery effluents which exhibit very high value for chromium, sulphide, and chloride, TDS, TSS, BOD and COD in the water stream or land. In the course of the last two decades a wide variety of technologies had been developed for cleanup operations of contaminated sites. Bioremediation has evolved as the most promising one because of its economical safety and environmental features, since organic contaminants become actually transferred and some of them are fully mineralized. Bioremediation of tannery effluents is an attractive environment friendly, safe and cost effective alternative technology to conventional methods. Microbes in the environment play an important role in cycling and destroying them through biodegradation (Aneez Mohamed *et al.*, 2011).

Bioremediation is pollution control technologies that use biological systems to catalyse the biodegradation or transformation of various toxic chemicals to less harmful forms. This natural process of bioremediation includes bioengineering, the capabilities of intrinsic microorganisms to clean-up the environment is an effective alternative to conventional remediation methods. Microbial treated industrial effluents contains an array of plant nutrients, trace elements, which is essential for plants like rice, maize and sugarcane for non- lodging and also for improving resistance to pests and diseases. Industrial wastes for land application have been proven to be a cost effective. The effects of various bioremediated industrial effluents, sludge materials and metal elements on seed germination, growth and yield of crop plants have captivated the attention of many workers (Rahman *et al.,* 2002; Selivanovskaya and Latypova, 2006; Yu and Gu, 2007; Giannis *et al.,* 2008).

OBJECTIVES OF THE PRESENT STUDY

1) To collect the tannery effluent and analysis of its physico – chemical characteristics.

2) To isolate and identify the bacteria and fungi from tannery effluent.

3) To screen the bacterial and fungal isolates based on reduction of physico-chemical characteristics and heavy metals reduction.

4) Bioremediation of tannery effluent by efficient microbial isolates and microbial consortium.

2. REVIEW OF LITERATURE

Environmental pollution is one of the major problems of the world and it is increasing day by day due to urbanization and industrialization. Over the last few decades large scale usage of chemicals in various human activities has very fast, particularly in a country like India which has to go for rapid industrialization in order to sustain over growing large problem of population (Mustafa *et al.*, 2010). Environmental pollution has been recognized as one of the major problems of the modern world. The problem of environmental pollution on account of essential industrial growth is practical terms, the problem of disposal of industrial water, whether solid, liquid or gaseous. All the three types of wastes have the potentially of ultimately polluting water (Barman *et al.*, 2000; Kisku *et al.*, 2000). Use of industrial effluent and sewage sludge on agricultural land has become a common practice in India as a result of which these toxic metals can be transferred and concentrated into plant tissues from the soil. These metals have damaging effects on plants themselves and may become a health hazard to man and animals. Above certain concentrations and over a narrow range, the heavy metals turned into toxins (Babich *et al.*, 1982).

Industrial effluents consist of organic compounds along with inorganic complexes and other non biodegradable substances. These pollutants alter the quality of ground water and soil (Karthikeyan *et al.,* 2010). Environmental pollution caused by heavy metals is increasing along with the increase in the usage of chemicals in industry and agriculture. Such pollution is apparent in streams and lakes and in ground water which was replenished directly from surface water (Huget *et al.*, 2009). The quality of life on earth is in extractable linked to overall quality in the environment. currently, there are two fundamental pollution related problems are the disposal of large quantities of wastes that are continually being produced and the removal of toxic compounds that have been accumulated at the dump sites in the soils and in water system over the last few decades (Hsua *et al.*, 2006). Uncontrolled urbanization has caused serious environmental pollution problems due to the disposal of sewage and industrial effluents to water bodies. Unlike many other pollutants, heavy metals are difficult to remove from the environment (Poornima *et al.,* 2014).

2.1. TANNING INDUSTRY

Tanning industry is recognized as a serious environmental threat all over the world. In India, leather industry contributes 15 per cent of the world total leather production (Alam *et al.*, 2009) and the fourth exchange earner with a share of around 7 per cent in the country's total exports. Tanning industry contributes significantly towards exports, employment generation and occupies an important role in Indian economy on the other hand; tannery wastes are ranked as the highest pollutants among all the industrial wastes (Soyaslan and Karaguzel, 2007).

De Nicola *et al.* (2007) stated that the trimming, soaking and fleshing the hide of any cattle, cow, goat, sheep, pig and horse are selected. The skin is carefully removed from the dead animals. To removed the meat and flesh from the hide, the skin is soaked in water for several hours. The preserved raw hides regain their normal water contents. Unhairing is done by chemical dissolution of hair and epidermis with an alkaline medium of sulphide and lime. After skinning at the slaughter house, the hide appears to contain excessive meat, fleshing usually precedes unhairing and liming.

Removal of hair on the hide quicklime was applied on the wet surfaces and rubbed. The unhaired, fleshed and alkaline hides are neutralized with acid ammonium salts and treated with enzymes, similar to those found in the digestive system. During the process hair roots and pigments are removed and hides become soft by the enzyme treatment (De Nicola *et al.*, 2007).

Global environmental regulation is challenging the leather processing industry. Tanning is a major small-scale industry in India (Das and Guha, 2007). The process of tanning involves the use of large amounts of fresh water and various chemicals. Every 10 kg of raw skins tanned requires about 350 litres of fresh water. Various chemicals used in tanning are lime, sodium bicarbonate, common salt, sodium sulphate, chrome sulphate, fat liquors, vegetable oils and dyes. The waste water discharged for 100 kg of skins and hides and skins processed, varies from 3000 litres to 3200 litres. The largest polluting material in the tanning industry which was very difficult to rid off is common salt. For every 10 tonnes of salted hides and skins processed, 2 - 3 tonnes of salt was removed and in addition another one ton of salt was removed, while pickling (Altaf *et al.*, 2008).

In tannery process pickling is done for preventing the rottened or stiffened and pickling increases the acidity of the hide to a pH of 3, enabling chromium tannins to enter the hide. Salts are added to prevent the hide from swelling. For preservation purposes, 0.03 – 2 weight percent fungicides and bactericides are applied. Soaked the hide in water for a whole night and the hide will be ready for tanning (Lefebvre *et al.*, 2006).

2.2. IMPACT OF TANNERY EFFLUENT TO THE ENVIRONMENT

The damages to the environment by the hazardous tannery effluent is becoming an acute problem in the country. The chrome tanning process results in toxic metals, especially chromium III passing to wastewater and are not easily eliminated by ordinary treatment process (Franco *et al.*, 2005). Tannery waste waters are mainly characterized by high salinity, high organic loading and specific pollutants such as chromium (Colak *et al.*, 2005).

The untreated tannery industrial effluents are often discharged into the water bodies. This contaminated water spread wide range of water borne diseases. The agricultural fields around these water bodies are affected (Chandra and Kulsheshtha, 2004). The impact of the tannery effluents is so stupendous that the water has become unfit for drinking and irrigation. The total dissolved solids of the ground water is 17,000 mg/l. (Waziri, 2006).

People working in pre-tanning and tannin department were prone to be exposed to chromium at a higher risk compared to the finishing department. Continual skin contact with organic solvents during wetting and finishing stage leads to defatting of the skin and eventual dermatitis. Aluminium sulphate and carbon black used as tanning agent and pigment respectively, causes respiratory disorders for the workers. Perchloroethane employed as degreasing agent causes narcosis and drowsiness. The white spirit is used in open drum tanning process of sheep skins which is flammable in nature (Zhang *et al.*, 2008).

Soil pollution by tannery industry released metals is essentially different from air or water pollution because the persistence of heavy metals in soil is reportedly much longer than in other compartments of the biosphere. Removal of heavy metals from polluted soil is difficult. Once deposited on the soil certain metals such lead and chromium may be virtually permanent (Okeyode and Moshood, 2010).

The tannery industries release heavy metals is a serious problem because of industrial activities and sewage sludge applications have largely contributed to the wide spread of these elements in the terrestrial environment (Viti *et al.*, 2003). The tannery industries released most commonly occurring metals at the discharge sites are lead, chromium, arsenic, zinc, cadmium, copper and mercury. The presence of these metals in the water and soil may cause serious threat to human health and ecological systems (Sundar *et al.*, 2010).

In Tamil Nadu, almost 50 per cent of the industries thrive in Palar river basin has been critically affected by the pollution caused by tannery industries. The effluent from the industries was discharged onto water bodies, road sides, agricultural fields and open lands. The salts present in the effluent seeped into the ground surface and thereby caused the pollution of ground water sources in the area. Contamination of the ground water has caused water scarcity, for agriculture as well as domestic purposes. The quality of water has degraded so much that crops no longer grow when irrigated by this water due to clogging of salts at the roots. Crops that were extensively grown in the river basin, thirty years ago, are no longer cultivated due to the absence of good quality water. As a result the income from the agriculture has subsided and most farmers are driven into the viscous circle of poverty (Shrey Kankaria *et al.*, 2011).

Untreated tannery waste water for irrigation on urban and sub-urban lands has long been practiced in several parts of the world due to its high contents of plant nutrients and due to lack of infrastructure facilities for safe disposal. The sewage effluents are not only a rich source of organic matter but also contain heavy metals like Fe, Mn, Cu, Zn, Pb, Cr and Ni. Continuous use of such effluents for crop production can result in accumulation of the metals in the soil as well as in plants, in concentrations that may become phytotoxic (Sangeetha *et al.,* 2012).

2.3. PHYSICO–CHEMICAL CHARACTERISTICS OF TANNERY EFFLUENTS

Tannery effluent is one of the most polluting industrial wastes (Sahasranaman and Buljan, 2000). Tannery industries generates large quantities of wastewater with ammonium, sulfates, surfactants, acids, dyes, sulfonated oils and organic substances, including natural or synthetic tannins. The chemical substances are applied to transform the animal skin into products with great capacities for dyeing, as well as to increased the mechanical and hydrothermal resistance. Considering that the greater part of these organic compounds are resistant to conventional chemical and biological treatments (Schrank *et al.*, 2005; Kurt *et al.*, 2007; Preethi *et al.*, 2009).

Tanneries discharges many toxic pollutants like sulfides, phenolic compounds, magnesium, sodium, potassium, chromium and other mineral salts, dyes and solvents. Chromium contributes a major share to the hazardous nature of tannery effluent (Jimenez *et al.,* 2009). Improper disposal of such hazardous tannery effluents is an acute problem and damaged the environment. (Shitole and Panvalkar, 2011).

Shanker *et al.* (2005) described that the tannery effluent contains chemicals such as sodium chloride, sodium sulfate, lime and chromium used at different stages of tanning process and the discharged effluent containing is non-permissible limits of chromium and proved to be phytotoxic. Chromium exists in limits in two oxidation states, trivalent chromium Cr (III) and hexavalent Chromium Cr (VI) both the forms are toxic to the plants and inhibit the germination, reduced the growth, generated the oxidative stress, decreased the protein content, inhibit the photosynthesis and alter enzyme activities in the exposed plants.

Sharma and Adholeya (2011) reported that water plays a vital role in tannery operations. Approximately, 30 - 40 litres of water were used for processing of one kilogram of raw hide/skin into finished leather. However, volume of effluent and its physico-chemical characteristics varies from tannery to tannery. Generally, the tanning wastes contain high COD, BOD and high amounts of chromium mostly in the trivalent form.

Kawser Ahmed *et al.* (2011) studied that the physico-chemical properties of tannery and textile effluents and water of adjacent river (Buriganga and Karnatoli, Dhaka) at three different locations. The physico-chemical properties such as Biological Oxygen Demand (BOD), Salinity, Total Dissolved Solid (TDS), Total Suspended Solid (TSS), Sodium (Na^+), Potassium (K^+), Calcium (Ca^{2+}), Iron (Fe^{3+}), Phosphate (PO), Chloride (Cl^-), Nitrite (NO) and Nitrate (NO_3) of tannery effluent were 92.12 - 100.6, 4.05 - 5.83, 3200 - 5355, 850 -1103.9, 1737.62 - 1835.0, 65.5 - 72, 188.5 - 273.1, 0.26 - 0.32, 50.85 - 66.88, 79.41 - 88.79, 0.66 - 1.22 and 0.48 - 4.63 mg/l, respectively. Sangeetha *et al.* (2012) investigated that the impact of diluted and undiluted tannery effluent on seed germination percentage and physiology of maize. Antioxidants were studied as biomarkers of the stress induced by treatment with effluent which contains chromium beyond the limits.

2.4. BIOREMEDIATION OF TANNERY INDUSTRIAL EFFLUENTS BY MICROBIAL ISOLATES

Trasar Cepeda *et al.* (2000) reported that lower microbial biomass and enzyme activities in areas polluted with tannery effluent, compared to unpolluted control areas in Spain. On the other hand, the microbial biomass increased in soils treated with tannery waste in Mexico (Alvarez-Bernal *et al.*, 2006). Barajas-Aceves *et al.* (2007) also observed that the tannery sludge stimulated soil microbial activity in Mexico. The microbial community structure based on PLFA profiling changed from Gram positive bacteria to Gram negative bacteria in heavily tannery waste polluted soils in Australia (Kamaludeen *et al.*, 2003). The results suggested that the more studies need to be conducted to assess the effects of tannery sludge of different origins on microbial communities under different soil and climatic conditions.

Bento *et al.* (2003) observed that the maximum chromium reduction was occured at the optimum pH (7 – 9) and temperature (30°C) by *Bacillus* sp. And they studied that the remediation of effluents using physical methods like activated charcoal, pH at different ranges and different time periods and biological methods using the aquatic weed hyacinth as a biological pollutant removal.

An *Arthrobacter* sp. and a *Bacillus* sp., isolated from a long-term tannery waste contaminated soil were examined for their tolerance to hexavalent chromium [Cr(VI)] and their ability to reduce Cr (VI) to Cr (III) a and detoxification process in cell suspensions and cell extracts. Both bacteria tolerated Cr (VI) at 100 mg/ml on a Minimal salts agar medium supplemented with 0.5 per cent glucose, but *Arthrobacter* could able to grow in liquid medium at this concentration. *Arthrobacter* sp. could reduced the Cr (VI) upto 50 µg/ml, while, *Bacillus* sp. was not able to reduced the Cr (VI) beyond 20 µg/ml. *Arthrobacter* sp. was distinctly superior to the *Bacillus* sp. in terms of their Cr(VI) reducing ability and resistance to Cr (VI). Assays with permeabilized (treated with toluene or Triton X 100) cells and crude extracts demonstrated that the Cr (VI) reduction was mainly associated with the soluble protein fraction of the cell. *Arthrobacter* sp. Which has a great potential for bioremediation of Cr(VI) containing waste (Meghara *et al.,* 2003).

Shaili Srivastava and Indu Shekhar Thakur (2006) observed *Aspergillus niger* isolated from soil of leather tanning effluent had higher activity to remove chromium in tannery effluent then the other fungal isolates.

The tannery effluent collected from Common Effluent Treatment Plant (CETP), Unnao (U.P., India) was toxic in nature, had high BOD, COD, TDS and Cr content (5.88 mg l-1). Several chromate tolerant bacteria had been isolated and characterized from the effluent (NBRIP-1, NBRIP-2, NBRIP-3 and NBRIP-4). Growth of the strains was reduced at higher Cr concentration with extention of lag phase. The strains had great potential in recovery and detoxification of Cr from tannery effluent Shukla *et al.,* (2007).

The reduction/detoxification of Cr(VI) to Cr (III) form were studied Acevedo-Aguilar *et al.,* 2006; Morales and Cristiani (2008) the chromium resistant bacteria of *Pseudomonas, Escherichia, Bacillus, Enterobacter, Microbacterium* and sulphate reducing bacteria (SRB) including *Desulfovibrio, Desulfomicrobium* and *Desulfotomaculum* are being studied extensively (Cheung and Gu, 2007). The most common problem encountered while working with bacterial systems is the harvesting of cells after treatment. On the other hand, fungal biomasses are easy to grow and produce high biomass and are comparatively easier to harvest.

Microorganisms including bacteria, fungi, algae and yeast are found to be efficiently accumulating heavy metal ions (Gadd *et al.,* 2010). Bacteria and fungi are the chief agents for biodegradation. A large number of studies for the removal of metal ions have been reported using strains of *Penicillium, Rhizopus* and *Aspergillus* (Kapoor *et al.,* 1999; Say *et al.,* 2004).

Varenyam Aclhal *et al.* (2011) remediated the chromium present in tannery effluent contaminated soil by a brown rot fungus chromium has become an important soil contaminated at may sites throughout the world and facilitating the reduction of toxic Cr(VI) to non toxic Cr(III) using different microorganisms such as bacteria and fungi was becoming attractive remediation strategy. There is a need to find out different fungal species that can remove such toxic heavy metal ions from contaminated sites. The potency of a brown rot fungus, *Gloeophyllum sepiarium* was evaluated to remediated the chromium contaminated soil for the first time. The contaminated soil sample containing fungal biomass was analyzed by Flame absorption spectrometer and soil nutrient analysis was also performed. The results of the study indicated that the removal of 94 per cent Cr(VI) by the fungal biomass determined by Atomic absorption spectrophotometry after 6 months. Also, *Gloeophyllum sepiarium* increased the contents of organic matter, carbon, nitrogen, and phosphorus present in the contaminated soil after its inoculation. The research showed that the fungal biosorption by brown rot fungi also have a potential to be used in the removal of heavy metal ions from the soils.

Seema Sharama *et al.* (2012) conducted the studies to isolated and characterized the Cr(VI) reducing bacteria from soil contaminated with tannery effluent and evaluated the bacteria for Cr(VI) reduction activity. A comparative growth and reduction studies were conducted in Acetate Minimal Media (AMM) in the tannery effluent to remove Cr(VI) from the tannery effluent and other contaminated environment. The results encouraged for the development of cost effective and user friendly bioremediation technology for tannery industry.

Priya Pillai *et al.* (2012) observed that development of an efficient and value added process for the management of chrome shavings, a protein rich, chromium containing solid waste, produced in large quantities during the post-tanning operations in the leather industry, using *Bacillus subtilis*, a hot spring isolate. This bacterium was able to effectively degrade and grow using chrome shavings as the protein source and produced in the spent medium high levels of a keratinolytic serine protease that can be proficiently applied for the pre-tanning processing step of hide dehairing. The bacterium was moderately chromium resistant tolerating upto 35 ppm and 350 ppm of Cr(VI) and Cr(III) salts, respectively and showed bioaccumulation and biosorption of Cr(III) and Cr(VI).

A large number of previous studies demonstrated that the bacteria were able to transform hexavalent chromium to less toxic trivalent chromium that is stabilized within soil rather than dissolved in groundwater. However, concern persists about the long term stability of the chromium in these insoluble forms. Angela *et al.* (2014) studies to determined the stability of chromium within soil after biotreatment. Laboratory columns packed with highly contaminated soil from a chromium plating site were used to simulate in situ conditions. Molasses, nitrate and sulfate were added to artificial groundwater in order to stimulated the naturally occurring bacteria in the soil to transform Cr(VI). Carbon consumption, nitrate reduction, and hydraulic conductivity decreases to provided the evidences of bioactivity as the main cause of reduced effluent Cr(VI) compared to columns without carbon and/or nitrate addition. Subsequent flushing of the bio stabilized soil for 12 – 15 days with un amended GW maintained effluent Cr(VI) below 100 mg/L compared to conditions without molasses addition where, the effluent Cr(VI) concentrations always exceeded 655 mg/L. In batch tests after biotreatment, the soil was equilibrated with three different types of aqueous solutions in order to determine the stability of the chromium. Equilibrium aqueous chromium concentrations were the lowest from the soil that was removed from columns treated with carbon and nitrate addition. The results demonstrated that the biological activity stimulated by carbon and nitrate addition resulted in significant chromium stabilization forms that were not readily desorbed from the soil.

Immobilized *Aspergillus niger* and *Aspergillus oryzae* have been used from effluents for the removal of cadmium, lead, nickel and chromium (Kapoor and Viraraghavan, 1998). Among the chromium resistant fungi, *Aspergillus* are being studied extensively (Gouda, 2000; Nouri *et al.*, 2005; Park *et al.*, 2005; Srivastava and Thakur, 2006; Acevedo Aguilar *et al.*, 2006; Congeevaram *et al.*, 2007; Mungasavalli *et al.*, 2007; Fukuda *et al.*, 2008). The other reported chromium resistant fungi are *Mucor* (Pillichshammer *et al.*, 1995; Tobin and Roux, 1998), *Rhizopus oryzae* (Park *et al.*, 2005), *Hirsutella* sp. (Srivastava and Thakur, 2006), *Cunninghamella elegans* (Prigione *et al.*, 2009), *Paecilomyces* sp. (Cardenas Gonzalez and Acosta Rodriguez, 2010; Sharma and Adholeya, 2011b), *Penicillium* (Fukuda *et al.*, 2008; Park *et al.*, 2005), *Trichoderma inhamatum* (Morales-Barrera and Cristiani, 2008).

2.5. RECYCLING OF MICROBIAL REMEDIATED TANNERY EFFLUENTS FOR AGRICULTURAL USE

Tannery effluent was reported to cause adverse effect on plant growth when used as such. In semi arid country like India there lies a threat of complete scarcity of water in future. All the river basins having deficient volume of water for irrigation, the effluent from industries can reduce the pressure on water scarcity for irrigation (Thirunavukarasu and Lourdraj, 2005). Effect of toxic chemicals on plants and environmental impact of tannery effluents on plant and animal kingdom has been extensively studied. The phytotoxic impact of the heavy metal was observed on crop such as cabbage, water chestnut, tomatoes, chillies and rice (Upreti *et al.*, 2004).

Tannery wastewater contains utilizable nutrients, but also toxic organic compounds which might affect soil processes and plant growth and pathogens, which might poses a threat to the local farming community. Tannery effluent was composted with cow manure and wheat straw for 90 days to reduces the pathogens and toxic organic compounds and monitored. The compost was characterized by an electrolytic conductivity (EC) of 28.1 ms cm^{-1}, cation exchange capacity of 17.7 meq 100 g^{-1}, an absorbance at 645 nm of 0.0175, a respiration rate of 0.062 mg CO2-C kg^{-1} compost-C day^{-1}, pH 8.5 and C:N ratio 7:1 with a germination index for cress (*Lepidium sativum*) of 48 per cent after 90 days. Less than 10 faecal coliforms and no *Salmonella* sp., *Shigella* sp. or eggs of helminthes were detected in the compost while, total coliforms decreased by log$_{10}$ of 2. Total concentrations of lead (Pb) were 8.9 mg kg^{-1} dry compost, chromium (Cr) 77 mg kg^{-1} dry compost, cadmium (Cd) 0.4 mg kg^{-1} dry compost, copper (Cu) 10.3 mg kg^{-1} dry compost and sodium (Na) 14,377 mg kg^{-1} of dry compost. The characteristics of compost indicated that it was mature, but the germination index for cress of less than 50per cent remaining phytotoxic compounds.

However, the large salt concentrations (especially Na), might have inhibited cress development and thus reduced the germination index (Contreras Ramos *et al.*, 2004.)

The metal accumulation potential of *Chenopodium album* L. grown on various amendments of Tannery Sludge (TS) was studied after 60 days of sapling planted. The analysis of the results showed that the levels of pH, cation exchange capacity, organic carbon, organic matter and DTPA (Diethylene Triamine Pentaacetic Acid) extractable metals of amendments increased by the addition of tannery sludge ratio. Shoot length of the plant increased by the addition of sludge, whereas, no marked change was observed in root length, fresh and dry weight of the plant. Accumulation of the metals in the plants was found in the order; Fe>Mn >Zn >Cr>Cu >Pb >Ni >Cd. Translocation of toxic metals (Cr, Pb, Cd) in different parts of the tested plant was found in the order of leaves> stems> roots. An increase in the photosynthetic pigments, carotenoid and leaf protein contents of the plants were found to increase with increased in sludge amendments. Correlation analysis between metal accumulation in the plants with DTPA extractable metals emphasized that Mn, Ni, Cr, Pb and Cd showed positive correlation ($p< 0.05$), whereas, Fe, Zn and Cu showed negative correlation. Transfer factor analysis emphasized that 10 per cent TS amendments were suitable for phytoextraction of Cr. Overall analysis of the data exhibited that the plants may be used for phytoextraction of Cr from tannery waste contaminated soil and most of the metal was accumulated in harvestable part which is a matter of serious concern, whenever used for edible purposes (Gupta and Sinha, 2007).

The impact of toxicity was evident as visible symptoms of like chlorosis, yellowing and immature fall of leaves, poor growth and retarded flower, fruit and green yields. Metabolic alterations by metal exposure have also been described in plants either by direct effect on enzymes or other metabolities. The imbalance of nutrients and nutritional disorders in the plants due to heavy metal interactions with plant nutrients (Chunillal *et al.*, 2005). A number of studies have been done on growth of plants using 10per cent, 20per cent, 25per cent, 50 per cent and 75per cent effluents. The effect of undiluted and diluted (50per cent) distillery effluent on seed germination and seedling growth of *Zea mays* and *Oryza sativa* was studied by (Pandey *et al.*, 2008).

HANAN SELMAN HASSAN

Khilji and Barbeen (2008) studied the growth pattern and accumulation of *Hydrocyte umbellate* on treatment with diluted tannery (20, 40 and 60%) sludge. When tannery effluent gains access to cultivable lands or when the lands are irrigated with effluent, the fertility of the soil is affected, it changes the characteristics of soil and interferes with intake of water by plants. Presence of chromium influences the metabolic processes of plants (Devarajan *et al.,* 1993).

Sharma and Adholeya (2011) reported that potential plant species are slow growing or having less biomass producing ability. Hence, the selection of plants which having fast growth and high biomass producing ability along with the ability to grow and remove heavy metal from the absolute contaminated soil/sludge conditions.

Sangeetha *et al.* (2012) studied that the effect of tannery effluent, which contained chromium beyond non-permissible limits on the antioxidant defenses of *Zea mays*. The seeds were treated with diluted (50 per cent) and undiluted tannery effluent and the alterations in the germination physiology and enzymic antioxidant levels were studied. The seed germination percentage and seedling growth remain unaltered in the treated seeds when compared to the controls. However, the levels of the enzymic antioxidants namely superoxide dismutase, catalase and glutathione peroxidase were significantly elevated. Zymogram analysis confirmed the enhanced activity of catalase in the seeds treated with undiluted effluent. There was also a significant increase in starch and protein content of the treated seeds.

3. MATERIALS AND METHODS

3.1 GENERAL METHODS

3.1.1 Cleaning of glasswares

All the glasswares were first soaked in cleaning solution (100 g of potassium dichromate was added to 100 ml of distilled water followed by addition of 50 ml of concentrated sulphuric acid) for about 12 hrs and washed in tap water. Finally, they were cleaned with distilled water, dried and used for the study.

3.1.2 Sterilization

All the media were sterilized in an autoclave at 15 lbs pressure for 20 minutes. The glasswares were sterilized at 160°C for 1 hrs in Hot air oven.

3.1.3. Chemicals

All the chemicals used in the experiments were of analytical reagents (AR) grade and distilled water was used throughout the study.

3.2. COLLECTION OF TANNERY EFFLUENT SAMPLES

The tannery effluent to be bioremediated was collected from Vaaniyambadi, Vellore district of Tamil Nadu, India. Before sampling the effluent, the polythene container was cleaned thoroughly using distilled water. Immediately after the effluent sampling, the effluent sample was taken to the laboratory and stored at room temperature in the laboratory for further analysis using standard methods.

3.3. ANALYSIS OF PHYSICO – CHEMICAL CHARACTERISTICS OF COLLECTED TANNERY EFFLUENT

3.3.1 Physical parameters

3.3.1.1 Colour

The colour of the collected tannery was observed visually.

3.3.1.2 Odour

The odour of the collected tannery effluent was categorized as pleasant or unpleasant by direct smelling of the sample.

3.3.1.3 Temperature

The temperature of the tannery effluent was noted using Thermometric method at the site of sampling using portable calibrated mercury thermometer (EPA, 1998).

3.3.1.4 pH

The pH of the tannery effluent was determined by Potentiometric method using pH meter already standardized by using buffer solutions of known value before analysis.

3.3.1.5. Electrical conductivity (EC)

Electrical conductivity is the measure of the ability of an aqueous solution or material to convey an electric current. This ability depends upon the presence of ions, their total concentration, mobility, valencey and temperature. Electrical conductivity was determined by conductivity meter following the procedure of Richard (1954).

3.3.1.6. Total Suspended solids (TSS)

Total suspended solids are the portion of solids that usually remains on the filter paper. Suspended solids consist of silt, clay, fine particles of organic and inorganic matter, which is regarded as a type of pollutant because water high in concentration of suspended solid may adversely affect growth and reproduction rates of aquatic fauna and flora. For TSS analysis, known amount of sample was filtered through the previously weighed filter paper. Filter paper was then dried at $103 - 105°C$. TSS was determined by using following formula (Anon, 1992).

$$TSS\ mg/L = (Final\ wt - Initial\ wt)/Amount\ of\ sample\ taken \times 1000$$

3.3.1.7. Total Dissolved Solids (TDS)

Total dissolved solids (TDS) are the measure of total inorganic salts and other substances that are dissolved in water. TDS was determined following the procedure of Richard (1954) by using Electrical Conductivity (EC) meter.

$$TDS\ (mg/L) = EC\ \mu s/cm \times 0.67$$

3.3.1.8. Total Hardness

For the analysis of total hardness in tannery effluent, 25 ml of sample was diluted to 50 ml with distilled water. One to two ml of buffer was added to give a pH of 10.0 to 10.1. One to two drops of indicator solution was added and titrate with EDTA titrant to change in colour from reddish tinge to blue. A sample volume that requires less than 15 ml EDTA titrant was selected and complete titration was done within 5 min after buffer addition. The EDTA titrant was standardized against standard calcium solution using the above procedure.

$$Total\ Hardness\ (mg\ CaCO_3/L) = \ A \times B \times 1000/\ ml\ sample$$

Where

A = ml EDTA titrated for sample

B = mg $CaCO_3$ equivalent to 1 ml EDTA titrant

3.3.1.9. Estimation of Biological Oxygen Demand (BOD)

Winklers iodometric method (AOAC, 2005)

Preparation of dilution water: 1.0 ml of calcium chloride, magnesium sulphate, ferric chloride and phosphate buffer solutions were added to one litre of aerated distilled water and mixed thoroughly. This is the standard dilution water, prepared freshly every time. Freshly settled raw sewage at 2.0 ml was added as seeding to one litre of dilution water. The test water samples were diluted with seeded dilution water sample (1%, 5% and 10%). Each dilution sample was taken in two sets of BOD bottles. In one set of flasks, DO was determined immediately while the other set was kept for incubation at 20°C for 5 days.

Determination of DO

To the contents of the BOD bottle 2.0 ml of magnesium sulphate solution and 2.0 ml of alkali-iodide-azide solution were added and mixed thoroughly. A brown precipitate was formed, which was allowed to settle completely leaving a clear supernatant liquid. Then, 2.0 ml of concentrated sulphuric acid was added along the sides of the bottle and mixed for complete dissolution. The contents were transferred to a 500 ml conical flask and titrated immediately against 0.025 N sodium thiosulphate using starch as an indicator.

Calculation for DO

Volume of 0.025 N sodium thiosulphate used in the titration = DO in mg/L

DO at 0°C 760 mm pressure = DO × 0.07 mg/L

Calculation for BOD

BOD (5 days at 20°C) = $(DO_0 - DO_5 - BC) \times 100$ per cent sample.

DO_0 = Initial DO

DO_5 = DO after 20°C incubation for 5 days

BC = Blank correction i.e., difference in DO of blank on the initial day and after 5 days incubation.

3.3.1.10. Estimation of Chemical Oxygen Demand (COD)

Titrimetric method (AOAC, 2005)

A refluxing flask of 250 ml capacity was used with a ground glass 24/40 neck fitted with a 300 mm double surface condenser to which, a glass cap was fitted. 50 ml of the sample was taken in the flask. Mercuric sulphate of suitable quantity was added such that the ratio of chloride content of the sample to mercuric sulphate was 1:10 (For this, chloride content of the sample was estimated). Then, 5 ml of sulphuric acid-silver sulphate reagent was added, dissolved the mercuric sulphate and cooled in cold water while mixing. 25 ml of 0.125 N potassium dichromate was pipetted into the flask and mixed. Few porcelain bits were added and the condenser was attached. The water circulation was started and refluxed for 2 hrs. After cooling, the contents of the flask was transferred and diluted to about 350 ml with distilled water. Then, 2 to 3 drops of ferroin indicator was added and titrated against 0.125 N ferrous ammonium sulphate solution. The end point was the sharp colour change from blue - green to reddish brown. A blank was conducted using 50 ml of distilled water instead of the sample.

Calculation

COD in mg/L = (Blank titre value - Sample titre value) × 0.125 × 1000 × 8 volume of the sample taken.

3.3.2. CHEMICAL PARAMETERS

Analysis of chemical parameters of tannery effluent was done by using Trimetric analysis. Briefly, Total hardness as $CaCO_3$ (Ca and Mg) was determined by titration of samples against EDTA and Chloride against $AgNO_3$.

3.3.2.1. Estimation of Carbonate and Bicarbonate:

Titrimetric method (Natarajan 1988)

Added 25ml of the sample and 25ml of distilled water in a 250ml conical flask. Added phenolphthalein indicator solution. If no pink colouration , it indicated phenolphthalein alkalinity. If pink colour appeared then titrated with sulphuric acid (0.02N), until the solution became colourless. Added 3 drops of mixed indicator solution in which phenolphthalein alkalinity had been determined and titrated against sulphuric acid (0.02N) to light pink colour.

Calculation
Volume of the sample taken = 25ml
Volume of 0.1N sulphuric acid used up to phenolphthalein end point = A ml
Volume of 0.1N sulphuric acid used up to methyl orange end point =B ml
Volume of 0.1N sulphuric acid required up to neutralize bicarbonate alone = (B-A) ml.

Carbonate

1.0ml of 0.1N sulphuric acid=0.003g of CO3

2 x A ml of 0.1N sulphuric acid =0.003 x 2 x Ag

Amount of carbonate per litre of sample=0.003 x 2 x 1000 x 1000/25m

Bicarbonate

1.0ml of 0.1N sulphuric acid = 0.0061g of HCO3.

(B-A)ml of 0.1N sulphuric acid = 0.0061x(B-A)g of HCO3

Amount of bicarbonate per litre of sample = 0.0061X(B-A) x 1000 x 1000/25mg

3.3.2.2 Estimation of Calcium and Magnesium

EDTA Titrimetric method (AOAC, 2005)

Fifty ml of the sample was pipetted and added with 2.0 ml of sodium hydroxide to produce a pH of 12 - 13 and mixed well. Then, 0.1 - 0.2 g of the indicator was added and titrated immediately with EDTA. The colour change from pink to purple is considered as the end point.

Calculation

$$\text{Calcium and Magnesium in mg/L} = \frac{\text{Vol of 0.02N EDTA (consumed in Ca + Mg titration)} \times N \times 500 \times 100}{10 \times 10}$$

3.3.2.3 Estimation of Chloride

Silver nitrate Titrimetric method (Jackson, 1973)

Three ml of aluminium hydroxide was added to a measured volume of the sample in a beaker. Stirred well and allowed to settle. The precipitate was filtered, washed with chloride free distilled water. 100 ml of the sample was pipetted out into a porcelain dish and the pH was adjusted to be in the range of 7 - 9.5 to which 1 ml of potassium chromate indicator solution was added. This was titrated against standard silver nitrate solution with constant stirring until a slight precipitate reddish colouration persisted. A blank was set by placing 100 ml chloride – free distilled water instead of sample.

Calculation

If the silver nitrate solution is exactly 0.0282 N,

Chloride mg/L = Volume of 0.0282 N consumed (sample - blank) × 1000

3.3.2.4. Estimation of Sodium and Potassium

Flame photometric method (Jackson, 1973)

The flame photometer was standardized before feeding the sample and zero reading was set using deionized water. Using the stock solutions of sodium and potassium, the reading was adjusted to 100 at their specific wavelengths. Then, the samples were fed in the flame photometer and noted the readings to get the amounts of sodium and potassium directly as milligrams per litre, by referring to the appropriate calibration curve.

3.3.2.5. Estimation of Fluoride
Ion selective electrode method (APHA, 2005)

Prepared a series of standards by diluting standard fluoride solution 5.0, 10.0 and 20.0ml with 100ml distilled water, these standards are equivalent to 0.5, 1.0,and 2.0 mg fluoride/l. Added equal volume of fluoride buffer to samples were, standardized and immerse the electrode are measured.

Calculation

Mg fluoride/l= µg fluoride/ml sample

3.3.2.6. Estimation of Nitrate
Nitrate electrode method (APHA, 2005)

Transferred 10 ml sample to a 50 ml beaker, added 10ml buffer solution and stirred with a magnetic stirrer. Measured standards and samples at the same temperature. Read concentration from calibration curve.

3.3.2.7. Estimation of Nitrite

Colorimetric method (APHA, 2005)

Sample pH which was not between 5 and 9 was adjusted to that range. To 50.0ml of sample added 2.0ml of colour reagent and mixed. After adding colour reagent to standard and sample, the absorbance was measured at 543nm.

Calculation

Prepare a standard curve by plotting absorbance of standard against NO2-N concentration.

3.3.2.8. Estimation of Sulphate

Turbidimetric method (AOAC, 2005)

A sample size of 100 ml was measured into an Erlenmeyer flask and added with 20 ml buffer solution with constant stirring to which a spoonful of barium chloride crystals were added. After stirring, the readings were taken in a spectrophotometer at 420 nm.

3. 3. 3. TRACE METAL ANALYSIS

The estimation of trace heavy metals such as for Cr, Zn, Cu, Pb, Ni in the industrial effluent and soil was performed as per Malik *et al*. (1984).

3.3.3.1 Estimation of Chromium, Zinc, Iron, Copper, Lead, Cadmium, Manganese and Nickel by Atomic Absorption Spectrophotometric (AAS) method

Three concentrations of each standard metal solution were selected to find out the expected metal concentration of a sample. Then, each standard was aspirated into flame and the absorbance was recorded. A calibration curve was prepared by plotting the absorbance of standards versus their concentrations. The estimations of chromium, copper, lead, zinc and nickel were done at the wavelengths of 357.9 nm (chromium, iron, copper and manganese), 324.7 nm (lead), 228.8 nm (cadmium) 248.3 nm (zinc) and 232.1 nm (nickel).

Calculation

The concentration of each metal ion was calculated in milligrams per litre, by referring to the appropriate calibration curve.

3.4. ENUMERATION OF MICROBIAL POPULATION IN TANNERY EFFLUENT

The tannery effluent sample was serially diluted upto 10^{-6} dilution to determine the bacterial, fungal and actinomycetes populations. 0.1 ml of the sample dilutions (10^{-5} and 10^{-6}) were spreaded (Spread plate technique) on sterile petriplates containing Nutrient agar (NA) medium for the growth of bacterial colonies at $37°C$ for 24 hrs. The sample dilutions 10^{-3} to 10^{-4} were spread on sterile petriplates containing Rose Bengal Agar medium (RBA) for the growth of fungal colonies at $28°C$ for 3 days in a room temperature. For enumeration of actinomycetes in tannery effluent, the dilutions from 10^{-4} to 10^{-5} were spreaded on sterile petriplates containing Kenknight's agar medium (KKA) for the growth of actinomycetes colonies at $30°C$ for 5 to 7 days. The numbers of bacterial, fungal and actinomycetes colonies in the respective plates were counted and calculated.

cfu/ml = Number of colonies counted × Amount of sample taken × Dilution factor

3.5. ISOLATION AND IDENTIFICATION OF BACTERIAL ISOLATES FROM TANNERY EFFLUENT

3.5.1. Isolation of bacteria from Tannery effluent

Pour plate technique was used for the isolation of bacteria from the tannery effluent collected from Vaaniyambadi, Vellore district, Tamil Nadu, India. In this method, 1 ml of sample was thoroughly mixed with 99 ml of sterile distilled water, and then it was serially diluted by following standard procedure upto concentration of 10^{-6}. Then, 1 ml of serially diluted samples from each concentration of samples were transferred to sterile petriplates and evenly distributed throughout the plates and sterile unsolidified Nutrient agar was poured and it was allowed to solidified. The Nutrient agar plates were incubated at $37°C$ for 24 hours. After incubation, the bacterial colonies were isolated from the plates.

3.5.2. Maintenance of bacterial isolates

Well grown bacterial colonies were picked and further purified by streaking. The isolated strains were maintained on Nutrient agar slants and stored at 4°C.

3.5.3. Identification of the bacterial isolates

Identification of the bacterial isolates was carried out by the routine bacteriological methods i.e.,

a) By the colony morphology

b) Preliminary tests like Gram staining, Capsule staining, Endospore staining, Motility, Catalase and Oxidase.

c) Plating on selective medium.

d) By performing biochemical tests.

3.6. SCREENING OF BACTERIAL ISOLATES FOR ITS HEAVY METAL RESISTANCE

3.6.1. Disc diffusion method

The isolated bacterial strains (*Pseudomonas* sp. (P1), *Proteus* sp., *Bacillus* sp., *Escherichia* sp., *Serratia* sp., *Pseudomonas* sp. (P2), *Staphylococcus* sp., *Enterobacter* sp., *Alcaligenes* sp. and *Micrococcus* sp.) were tested for their resistance to heavy metals (Cr^{2+}, Zn^{2+}, Pb^{2+}, Cu^{2+} and Ni^{2+}) by Disc diffusion method. Freshly prepared Muller Hinton agar (MHA) plates were seeded with respective cultures individually. The disc impregnated (20 µl) with respective metal solution (100 mg/L metal solution of Cr^{2+}, Zn^{2+}, Pb^{2+}, Cu^{2+} and Ni^{2+}) were placed on the four corners of each petridishes and suitable control disc was also placed. The plates were then incubated at $28 \pm 2°C$ for 24 hrs. After incubation, the presence of inhibition zone was visualized. A zone size less than 1 mm was considered as resistance strain (Cervantes *et al.*, 1986). The bacterial isolates resistant to all the metals used were taken for further study.

3.6.2. Determination of Minimum Inhibitory concentration (MIC) (Cervantes *et al.*, 1986)

The Minimum inhibitory concentration (MIC) of heavy metal resistant bacterial isolates (*Pseudomonas* sp. (P1), *Proteus* sp., *Bacillus* sp., *Escherichia* sp., *Serratia* sp., *Pseudomonas* sp. (P2), *Staphylococcus* sp., *Enterobacter* sp., *Alcaligenes* sp. and *Micrococcus* sp.) grown on heavy metals (Cr^{2+}, Zn^{2+}, Pb^{2+}, Cu^{2+} and Ni^{2+}) incorporated media was determined by gradually increasing the concentration of the heavy metal by 10 µg/ml each time in the specific media until the strains failed to give colonies on the plate. The starting concentration used was 50 µg/ml. The culture growing on the last concentration was transferred to the higher concentration by streaking on the plate. The MIC was noted when the isolates failed to grow on plates.

3.7. BIOREMEDIATION OF HEAVY METALS IN TANNERY EFFLUENT USING BACTERIAL ISOLATES

Preparation of Heavy metal solution

The stock solutions of the heavy metals were prepared by mixing 100 mg of respective heavy metal *viz.*, Cr^{2+}, Zn^{2+}, Ni^{2+}, Cu^{2+} and Pb^{2+} in one litre of deionized water (Semra Ilhan *et al.*, 2004).

3.7.1. Heavy metal adsorption by living microbial cells (Bioaccumulation) (Vargas *et al.*, 2009)

About 1% living bacterial biomass (*Pseudomonas* sp. (P1), *Proteus* sp., *Bacillus* sp., *Escherichia* sp., *Serratia* sp., *Pseudomonas* sp. (P2), *Staphylococcus* sp., *Enterobacter* sp., *Alcaligenes* sp. and *Micrococcus* sp) were suspended individually in a solution (100 ml) supplemented with heavy metals for different pH, temperature, biomass concentration and carbon sources as described above. After incubation, cells were harvested by centrifugation. The supernatants of the samples were analysed and the quantity of each metal removed was measured using AAS and expressed as mg/L.

3.7.2. Heavy metal adsorption by dead microbial cells (Biosorption) (Vargas *et al.*, 2009)

Biomass from the bacterial isolates (*Pseudomonas* sp. (P1), *Proteus* sp., *Bacillus* sp., *Escherichia* sp., *Serratia* sp., *Pseudomonas* sp. (P2), *Staphylococcus* sp., *Enterobacter* sp., *Alcaligenes* sp. and *Micrococcus* sp) grown in Nutrient broth were harvested by centrifugation and washed with distilled water three times. The pellet was dried and milled. Aliquots of dried microbial cells (200 mg/L) were prepared in distilled water and homogenized in a mixer to destroy aggregated cells. About 1 ml of cell suspensions were added to the metal solution (100 ml) prepared and incubated. After incubation, the suspensions were centrifuged and filtered for biomass removal. Heavy metal concentration in the supernatant was measured as previously described.

3.7.3. Heavy metal adsorption by immobilized microbial cells (Johncy Rani *et al.*, 2010)

The bacterial cells (*Pseudomonas* sp. (P1), *Proteus* sp., *Bacillus* sp., *Escherichia* sp., *Serratia* sp., *Pseudomonas* sp. (P2), *Staphylococcus* sp., *Enterobacter* sp., *Alcaligenes* sp. and *Micrococcus* sp.) were immobilized as beads according to the procedure of Leung *et al.* (2000). Two percent sodium alginate solution is prepared in sterile distilled water by heating it to $60^{\circ}C$ and mixing it thoroughly on a magnetic stirrer. Later, 100 ml of the sodium alginate was cooled to room temperature and 10% (10 ml culture in 100 ml sodium alginate solution) of the cell culture was added, the optimum condition was also studied as described above. The contents were mixed well by vigorous shaking to get a homogenized mixture. In a separate beaker, 100 ml of 0.1 M calcium chloride solution was taken. The sodium alginate containing cell culture suspension was extruded drop wise through a syringe and allowed to fall in the beaker containing calcium chloride solution. The beads of sodium alginate gel formed are left in the beaker overnight for hardening. Then beads were washed and stored in distilled water at $28 \pm 2^{\circ}C$. One gram of material contained 16 to 17 beads, each bead approximately weighing 60 mg.

The beads (1 g) containing $>10^5$ cfu/ml biomass were added to the conical flask containing 50 ml of samples and incubated at room temperature for 72 hrs. After which, the samples were withdrawn for heavy metal analysis using AAS.

3.8. SPECIES LEVEL IDENTIFICATION OF BACTERIAL ISOLATES BY 16S rRNA SEQUENCING

The species level identification of bacteria which was isolated from tannery effluent was done by Phylogenetic analysis (16S rRNA Sequencing). 16SrRNA analysis was done by using predetermined universal primers of 16SrRNA. DNA isolated from pure culture was used as template. PCR was performed with a 50 µl reaction mixture containing primer 16S, DNA template buffer, $MgCl_2$, dXTPs, Taq polymerase. PCR products were analysed by electrophoresis in 1.8% agarose gel. PCR program was carried out in PTC-200 Peltier thermocycler.

RNA sequences were compared with already submitted sequence in database BLAST software. Further, most similar sequences were aligned by ClustalW and ClustalX software and Phylogenetic tree was drawn using PHYLIP software to analyze evolutionary relationships among sequences of isolated microorganism and nearest neighbours (Fulekar and Sharma, 2008).

3.9. OPTIMIZATION FOR HEAVY METAL REMOVAL BY BACTERIAL ISOLATES

Temperature, pH, biomass, heavy metal concentrations are the factors which affects the bioremediation process. Particularly, effect of pH, temperature (Kiran *et al.*, 2005), carbon sources, nitrogen sources, biomass concentration and incubation period (Gong *et al.*, 2007) on bioremediation (immobilized cells) experiments were investigated by optimization process. The effective bacterial isolates (*Bacillus subtilis*, *Serratia marcescens* and *Pseudomonas fluorescens*) were prepared as consortium in alginate beads. The alginate beads (1 g) of individual isolates and consortium for effluent and contaminated soil studies were added to the prepared metal solution and adsorption of metals was investigated for different pH (6, 7 and 8), temperature ($25°C$, $30°C$, $40°C$), carbon sources (glucose, sucrose, maltose and dextrose), nitrogen sources (peptone, yeast extract, ammonium nitrate and ammonium chloride) at one per cent level and incubation period (12 hrs, 18 hrs, 24 hrs and 30 hrs). The effect of biomass concentration was also tested at various levels *viz.*, 2 per cent, 3 per cent, 4 per cent and 5 per cent by adding calculated quantities of the culture in the medium and incubating them in a rotary shaker of 150 rpm for 72 hrs. The analyses of heavy metals were carried out by Atomic adsorption spectrophotometer (Perkin-Elmer) at 0.01 ppm sensitivity level after dilution of the samples.

3.10. SURVIVAL OF EFFICIENT BACTERIAL ISOLATES AND CONSORTIUM IN SODIUM ALGINATE BEADS

The viability of efficient bacterial isolates in alginate beads was observed by dissolving 1.0 g of alginate beads in 1.0 ml of respective broth containing 9.0 ml of potassium phosphate buffer (0.25 M, pH 6.8) in a test tube for 16 - 24 hrs at $28 \pm 2^{\circ}$C. Further, the growth of the bacterial isolates was observed by pour plate technique. The viability test was carried out following serial dilution technique with freshly prepared alginate beads and as well as alginate beads stored at 4°C at an interval of 1 month upto a period of 6 months of study (Pankaj Trivedi and Anita Pandey, 2007).

3.11. BIOREMEDIATION OF TANNERY EFFLUENT USING IMMOBILIZED EFFICIENT BACTERIAL ISOLATES AND CONSORTIUM UNDER AEROBIC CONDITION

The collected tannery effluent was inoculated with immobilized beads containing efficient bacterial consortium (*Bacillus subtilis*, *Serratia marcescens* and *Pseudomonas fluorescens*), and air was passed continuously using an aerator. After 3 and 6 months, the sample were filtered under aseptic condition and physico - chemical parameters were estimated. The bioremediated effluent was later used for irrigation during field study.

4. RESULTS

4.1. ANALYSIS OF PHYSICO - CHEMICAL PROPERTIES OF TANNERY EFFLUENT

The physico – chemical characteristics of the tannery effluent collected from Vaniyambadi region, Tamil Nadu, India was analyzed and the results were furnished in Table – 1. The tannery effluent was acidic in nature with brown colour and emitted unpleasant smell. The temperature of collected tannery effluent was 38°C and the EC was 30.2 dSm^{-1}. The hardness of the tannery effluent was recorded as 5200 mg/L. The Total Suspended Solid (TSS) and Total Dissolved Solid (TDS) present in collected tannery effluent were 316 mg/L and 1500 mg/L respectively. It also showed high value of Biological oxygen demand (BOD) (1280 mg/L) and Chemical oxygen demand (COD) (2037 mg/L). High amount of chloride (1464 mg/L), Calcium (160 mg/L), Magnesium (57 mg/L), Sodium (188 mg/L), Potassium (603 mg/L), Fluoride (6.0 mg/L), Nitrate (45 mg/L), Nitrite(33 mg/L), Sulphate (349 mg/L) and the toxic heavy metals (Cr^{2+}-146 mg/L, Ni^{2+}-57 mg/L, Zn^{2+}- 36 mg/L, Cu^{2+}- 29 mg/L, Fe^{2+}- 19.00 mg/ L, Cd^{2+}- 5.4 mg/L, Pb^{2+}- 4.6 mg/L and Mn^{2+}- 9.9 mg/L) were recorded in the collected tannery effluent sample.

Table - 1: Physico-chemical properties of collected Tannery effluent

Parameters	Raw Effluent	BIS Limit Is 2490-2009
Colour	Brown	-
Odour	Offensive	-
Temperature	38°C	-
pH	9.7	5.5 - 9.0
Electrical conductivity (dsm^{-1})	30.2	NM
Total hardness (mg/L)	5200	100
Total suspended solids (mg/L)	316	100
Total dissolved solids (mg/L)	1500	2100
Biological Oxygen Demand (mg/L)	1280	30
Chemical Oxygen Demand (mg/L)	2037	250
Carbonate (mg/L)	860	600
Bicarbonate (mg/L)	1428	NM
Calcium (mg/L)	160	200
Magnesium (mg/L)	57	30-100
Chloride (mg/L)	1464	1000
Sodium (mg/L)	188	NM
Potassium (mg/L)	603	NM
Fluoride (mg/L)	6.0	2.0
Nitrate (mg/L)	45	100
Nitrite (mg/L)	33	10
Sulphate (mg/L)	349	1000
Chromium (mg/L)	146	0.5
Nickel(mg/L)	57	3.0
Zinc (mg/L)	36	-
Copper(mg/L)	29	3.0
Iron (mg/L)	19	-
Cadmium (mg/L)	5.4	2.0
Lead (mg/L)	4.6	0.1
Manganese (mg/L)	9.9	-

TNPCB- Tamil Nadu Pollution Control board

HANAN SELMAN HASSAN

4.2. ENUMERATION OF MICROBIAL POPULATION IN TANNERY EFFLUENT

The number of microbial isolates (bacteria, fungi and actinomycetes) present in the collected tannery effluent was enumerated and the results were showed in Table – 2. The population of bacterial isolates was very high followed by fungal isolates and actinomycetes isolates. For bacteria, the dilutions from 10^{-1} to 10^{-4} showed too numerous bacterial count (i.e., more than 300 colonies). The bacterial count in 10^{-5} and 10^{-6} was 28.6×10^{5} and 19.1×10^{6} respectively. The fungal population was 10^{-3} (7.2×10^{3}) and 10^{-4} (6.8×10^{4}). The dilutions 10^{-5} and 10^{-6} showed too least fungal count (i.e., less than 30 colonies). In actinomycetes, the population was high in 10^{-1} followed by 10^{-2} and 10^{-3}. The dilutions 10^{-4}, 10^{-5} and 10^{-6} showed too least actinomycetes count.

4.3. IDENTIFICATION OF BACTERIA ISOLATED FROM TANNERY EFFLUENT

Ten different bacteria were identified from the tannery effluent and the characteristics of the bacterial isolates were recorded in Table – 3 to Table – 4. Ten different bacterial isolates were isolated and identified by staining techniques, motility test, platting on selective medium and biochemical tests. The isolated bacterial isolates were identified *Pseudomonas* sp. (P1)., *Proteus* sp., *Bacillus* sp., *Escherichia coli, Serratia* sp., *Pseudomonas* sp. (P2)., *Staphylococcus* sp., *Enterobacter* sp., *Alcaligenes* sp. and *Micrococcus* sp.

Table – 2: Enumeration of microbial population in collected Tannery effluent

S. No	Microorganisms	Dilutions	Microbial population (cfu ml^{-1})
1	Bacteria	10^{-5}	28.6×10^5 (6.45)
		10^{-6}	19.1×10^6 (7.28)
2	Actinomycetes	10^{-4}	-
		10^{-5}	-
3	Fungi	10^{-3}	7.2×10^3 (4.25)
		10^{-4}	6.8×10^4 (5.16)

Isolate No.	Gram staining	Shape	Spores	Motility	Nutrient agar	Mac Conkey agar	EMB Agar	MSA Agar	*Pseudomas* isolation agar	Growth at 42°C
TEB– 1	-	Rods	-	-	Red pigmented colonies	LF	-	-	-	-
TEB – 2	-	Rods	-	+	Swarming motility and fishy odour	NLF	-	-	-	-
TEB – 3	+	Rods	+	-	Large, circular and white colonies	NLF	-	-	-	-
TEB -4	-	Rods	-	+	Circular and colourless colonies	LF	Green metallic sheen observed	-	-	-
TEB -5	+	Cocci	-	-	Smooth, golden yellow colonies	LF	-	Golden yellow colonies	-	-
TEB -6	-	Rods	-	+	Fluorescent pigmented colonies	NLF	-	-	No bluish green colonies	-
TEB -7	-	Rods	-	+	Bluish green colonies	NLF	-	-	Bluish green colonies	+
TEB -8	-	Rods	-	-	Mucoid and cream colonies	NLF	-	-	-	-
TEB -9	-	Rods	-	+	Light cream colour colonies	NLF	-	-	-	-
TEB -10	+	Cocci	-	+	White colour colonies	LF	-	-	-	-

TEB –Tannery effluent bacteria; + - Positive; - - Negative; NLF – Non lactose fermenting colonies; LF – Lactose fermenting colonies

Table - 4: Biochemical characteristics of bacteria isolated from Tannery effluent

Isolate No.	Sugar fermentation (Acid/Gas)						Catalase	Oxidase	Gelatinase	Caseinase	Starch	Nitrate reduction	Urease	Indole	MR	VP	Citrate	Lipase	Pectinase	DNase	Coagulase
	Glucose	Sucrose	Mannitol	Mannose	Arabinose	Dextrose															
TEB – 1	+/-	+/-	+/-	+/-	-	-	+	-	+	+	-	-	-	+	+	+	+	-	-	-	-
TEB – 2	+/+	-	-	-	-	-	+	-	-	-	-	-	+	-	-	-	+	-	-	-	-
TEB – 3	+/-	-	+/-	-	-	-	+	-	+	-	+	+	-	-	-	+	+	-	-	-	-
TEB -4	+/+	+/+	+/+	-	-	-	+	-	-	-	-	-	-	+	+	-	-	-	-	-	-
TEB -5	+/-	+/-	+/-	-	-	+/-	-	-	-	-	-	-	-	-	-	+	+	-	-	+	+
TEB -6	+/-	-	+/-	+/-	+/-	-	+	+	+	+	-	-	+	-	-	-	+	-	+	-	-
TEB -7	+/+	-	-	-	-	-	+	+	+	+	-	-	+	-	-	-	+	+	-	-	-
TEB -8	+/-	+/-	+/-	-	-	-	+	-	-	-	-	-	+	-	+	-	+	-	-	-	-
TEB -9	+/-	+/-	+/-	-	-	-	+	+	-	-	-	-	-	-	-	-	+	-	-	-	-
TEB -10	+/-	+/-	+/-	+/-	-	+	+	+	+	-	-	+	-	-	-	-	+	-	-	-	-

TEB –Tannery effluent bacteria; + - Positive; - - Negative; +/+ - Acid/Gas; +/- - Acid/ No gas; A/A – Acid butt and alkali slant; A/A – Acid butt and acid slant; K/K – Alkali butt and Alkali slant; H_2S^- - No Hydrogen sulphide production; H_2S^+ - Hydrogen sulphide production; G^+- Gas produced; G^- - Gas not produced; TEB–1 *Serratia* sp; TEB-2 *Proteus* sp.; TEB-3 –*Bacillus* sp; TEB-4 *Escherichia* sp.; TEB-5 –*Staphylococcus* sp.; TEB-6 – *Pseudomonas* sp. (P1) , TEB-7 – *Pseudomonas* sp. (P2); TEB-8 – *Enterobacter* sp.TEB-9 –*Alcaligenes* sp.; TEB-10 –*Micrococcus* sp.

4.4. SCREENING OF BACTERIAL ISOLATES FOR ITS HEAVY METAL RESISTANCE

4.4.1. Determination of heavy metal resistant bacterial isolates by Disc diffusion method

The resistance of bacterial isolates *Pseudomonas* sp. (P1), *Proteus* sp., *Bacillus* sp., *Escherichia* sp., *Serratia* sp., *Pseudomonas* sp. (P2), *Staphylococcus* sp., *Enterobacter* sp., *Alcaligenes* sp. and *Micrococcus* sp. which were isolated from the tannery effluent was tested against toxic heavy metals (Cr^{2+}, Zn^{2+}, Ni^{2+}, Cu^{2+} and Pb^{2+}) by Disc diffusion method and the results were recorded in Table -5. All the ten bacterial isolates *viz.*, *Pseudomonas* sp. (P1), *Proteus* sp., *Bacillus* sp., *Escherichia* sp., *Serratia* sp., *Pseudomonas* sp. (P2), *Staphylococcus* sp., *Enterobacter* sp., *Alcaligenes* sp. and *Micrococcus* sp. were resistant to all the heavy metals.

4.4.2. Determination of Minimum Inhibitory Concentration (MIC) of bacterial isolates to heavy metals

The minimum inhibitory concentration (MIC) of bacterial isolates (*Pseudomonas* sp. (P1), *Proteus* sp., *Bacillus* sp., *Escherichia* sp., *Serratia* sp., *Pseudomonas* sp. (P2), *Staphylococcus* sp., *Enterobacter* sp., *Alcaligenes* sp. and *Micrococcus* sp.) to heavy metals (Cr^{2+}, Zn^{2+}, $Ni^{2+,}$ Cu^{2+} and Pb^{2+}) was determined and the results were showed in Table – 6. The bacterial isolates showed high tolerance to Chromium as compared with other heavy metals. Among the bacterial isolates, *Bacillus* sp. showed highest heavy metal tolerance (280 µg/ml for Cr^{2+} and 260 µg/ml for Zn^{2+} and Ni^{2+} 250 µg/ml, 240 µg/ml for Cu^{2+} and 210 µg/ml for Pb^{2+}) followed by *Serratia* sp., *Pseudomonas* sp. (P1), *Pseudomonas* sp. (P2), *Enterobacter* sp., *Escherichia coli*, *Alcaligenes* sp., *Micrococcus* sp. and *Proteus* sp. The bacterial isolate *Staphylococcus* sp. showed lowest heavy metal tolerance (130 µg/ml for Cr^{2+} and 100 µg/ml for Zn^{2+}, 120 µg/ml for Ni^{2+}, 100 µg/ml for Cu^{2+} and 100 µg/ml for Pb^{2+}) for all heavy metals.

Table – 5: Screening of bacterial isolates for its heavy metal resistance

S. No	Bacterial Isolates	Heavy Metals (100 mg/L)				
		Cr (VI)	Zn (II)	Ni (II)	Cu (II)	Pb (II)
1.	*Pseudomonas* sp. (P1)	R	R	R	R	R
2.	*Proteus*	R	R	R	R	R
3.	*Bacillus* sp.	R	R	R	R	R
4.	*Escherichia* sp.	R	R	R	R	R
5.	*Serratia* sp.	R	R	R	R	R
6.	*Pseudomonas* sp. (P2)	R	R	R	R	R
7.	*Staphylococcus* sp.	R	R	R	R	R
8.	*Enterobacter* sp.	R	R	R	R	R
9.	*Alcaligenes* sp.	R	R	R	R	R
10.	*Micrococcus* sp.	R	R	R	R	R

Table - 6: Determination of MIC of bacterial isolates to heavy metals

S. No.	Microbial Isolates	MIC (µg/ml)				
		Cr (VI)	Zn (II)	Ni (II)	Cu (II)	Pb (II)
1.	*Pseudomonas* sp. (P1)	270	250	250	210	220
2.	*Proteus*	160	140	120	100	110
3.	*Bacillus* sp.	280	260	250	240	210
4.	*Escherichia* sp.	180	170	160	160	130
5.	*Serratia* sp.	130	100	120	100	100
6.	*Pseudomonas* sp. (P2)	200	210	190	180	190
7.	*Staphylococcus* sp.	230	230	210	200	220
8.	*Enterobacter* sp.	190	180	170	140	150
9.	*Alcaligenes* sp.	180	170	160	140	160
10.	*Micrococcus* sp.	180	150	170	140	110

4.5. BIOREMEDIATION OF HEAVY METALS IN TANNERY EFFLUENT USING BACTERIAL ISOLATES

Bioremediation (Bioaccumulation, Biosorption and Immobilization) of heavy metals (Cr^{2+}, Zn^{2+}, Ni^{2+}, Cu^{2+} and Pb^{2+}) was studied by using live bacterial cultures, inactivated or dead bacterial cells and immobilized beads. Ten different bacterial isolates showed resistance against toxic heavy metals were used for the bioremediation studies. The results revealed that all the organisms were found to be effective in remedying heavy metals.

4.5.1. Heavy metal adsorption by living bacterial cells (Bioaccumulation)

The heavy metal adsorption by living bacterial cells was studied and the results were showed in Table − 7. The bioaccumulation studies revealed that the highest heavy metals adsorption was showed by the bacteria *Bacillus* sp. (58.5 mg/L for Cr^{2+}, 58.1 mg/L for Zn^{2+}, 57.3 mg/L for Ni^{2+}, 57.8 mg/L for Cu^{2+} and 54.2 mg/L for Pb^{2+}) followed by *Serratia* sp., *Pseudomonas* sp (P1), *Pseudomonas* sp. (P2), *Enterobacter* sp., *Escherichia* sp., *Alcaligenes* sp., *Micrococcus* sp. and *Proteus* sp., whereas, *Staphylococcus* sp. showed the lowest activity of heavy metal adsorption (33.2 mg/L for Cr^{2+}, 33.0 mg/L for Zn^{2+}, 32.6 mg/L for Ni^{2+}, 32.8 mg/L for Cu^{2+} and 30.4 mg/L for Pb^{2+}).

4.5.2. Heavy metal adsorption by dead microbial cells (Biosorption)

The heavy metal adsorption by dead bacterial cells was tested and the results were showed in Table − 8. Among the ten bacterial isolates, *Bacillus* sp. showed the highest heavy metal adsorption (70.4 mg/L for Cr^{2+}, 69.6 mg/L for Zn^{2+}, 70.3 mg/L for Ni^{2+}, 68.9 mg/L for Cu^{2+} and 64.6 mg/L for Pb^{2+}) followed by *Serratia* sp. , *Pseudomonas* sp. (P1), *Pseudomonas* sp. (P2), *Enterobacter* sp., *Escherichia* sp., *Alcaligenes* sp., *Micrococcus* sp. and *Proteus* sp. The bacterial isolate *Staphylococcu* sp. showed the lowest adsorption of the heavy metals (42.4 mg/L for Cr^{2+}, 43.5 mg/L for Zn^{2+}, 42.2 mg/L for Ni^{2+}, 40.8 mg/L for Cu^{2+} and 39.8 mg/L for Pb^{2+}).

4.5.3. Heavy metal adsorption by Immobilized bacterial cells

The heavy metal adsorption by immobilized bacterial isolates was analyzed and the results were showed in Table – 9. Among the ten bacterial isolates, *Bacillus* sp., showed maximum heavy metal adsorption (79.2 mg/L for Cr^{2+}, 78.4 mg/L for Zn^{2+}, 77.4 mg/L for Ni^{2+}, 76.8 mg/L for Cu^{2+} and 74.2 mg/L for Pb^{2+}) followed by *Serratia* sp., *Pseudomonas* sp. (P1), *Pseudomonas* sp. (P2), *Enterobacter* sp., *Escherichia* sp., *Alcaligenes* sp*., Micrococcus* sp*., and Proteus* sp., while *Staphylococcus* sp., showed the least heavy metal adsorption (50.4 mg/L for Cr^{2+}, 50.9 mg/L for Zn^{2+}, 50.0 mg/L for Ni^{2+}, 49.8 mg/L for Cu^{2+} and 47.4 mg/L for Pb^{2+}).

Table - 7: Heavy metal adsorption by living bacterial cells (Bioaccumulation)

S. No	Living bacterial cells	Heavy metals absorbed (Initial concentration – 100 mg/L)				
		Cr(VI)adsorbed (mg/L)	Zn(II) adsorbed (mg/L)	Ni(II) adsorbed (mg/L)	Cu(II) adsorbed (mg/L)	Pb(II) adsorbed (mg/L)
1.	*Bacillus* sp.	58.5	58.1	57.3	57.8	54.2
2.	*Serratia* sp.	56.6	55.3	54.6	54.2	52.8
3.	*Pseudomonas* sp. (P1)	53.2	51.8	51.3	51.6	50.2
4.	*Pseudomonas* sp. (P2)	51.3	50.8	50.6	49.8	47.4
5.	*Enterobacter* sp.	46.4	47.4	47.2	46.8	44.8
6.	*Alcaligenes* sp.	43.2	43.0	42.4	41.6	40.8
7.	*Escherichia* sp.	42.6	41.5	40.6	40.0	38.7
8.	*Micrococcus* sp.	38.6	38.4	36.3	36.6	34.5
9.	*Proteus* sp.	36.4	36.9	35.8	35.2	33.0
10.	*Staphylococcus* sp.	33.2	33.0	32.6	32.8	30.4
	SEd	2.74	2.64	2.70	2.72	2.68
	CD (P = 0.05)	5.49	5.29	5.42	5.46	5.38

Table - 8: Heavy metal adsorption by dead bacterial cells (Biosorption)

S.No	Dead bacterial cells	Heavy metals absorbed (Initial concentration – 100 mg/L)				
		Cr(VI) adsorbed (mg/L)	Zn(II) adsorbed (mg/L)	Ni(II) adsorbed (mg/L)	Cu(II) adsorbed (mg/L)	Pb(II) adsorbed (mg/L)
1.	*Bacillus* sp.	70.4	69.6	70.3	68.9	64.6
2.	*Serratia* sp.	67.6	67.3	65.8	65.2	63.8
3.	*Pseudomonas* sp. (P1)	64.8	63.6	64.4	62.6	60.4
4.	*Pseudomonas* sp. (P2)	63.0	61.7	61.8	60.4	58.6
5.	*Enterobacter* sp.	58.8	57.5	56.3	57.4	56.8
6.	*Alcaligenes* sp.	53.4	53.8	52.5	51.4	51.8
7.	*Escherichia* sp.	52.8	50.4	50.6	50.2	48.8
8.	*Micrococcus* sp.	48.9	48.4	46.2	47.8	46.4
9.	*Proteus* sp.	45.2	46.2	44.0	45.4	40.0
10.	*Staphylococcus* sp.	42.4	43.5	42.2	40.8	39.8
	SEd	3.05	2.88	3.11	2.92	2.90
	CD (P = 0.05)	6.12	5.78	6.24	5.86	5.82

Table - 9: Heavy metal adsorption by immobilized bacterial cells (Immobilization)

S. No	Immobilized bacterial cells	Heavy metals absorbed (Initial concentration – 100 mg/L)				
		Cr(VI)adsorbed (mg/L)	Zn(II) adsorbed (mg/L)	Ni(II) adsorbed (mg/L)	Cu(II) adsorbed (mg/L)	Pb(II) adsorbed (mg/L)
1.	*Bacillus* sp.	79.2	78.4	77.4	76.8	74.2
2.	*Serratia* sp.	75.6	74.8	72.3	72.3	71.4
3.	*Pseudomonas* sp. (P1)	73.2	70.3	71.0	69.8	68.4
4.	*Pseudomonas* sp. (P2)	70.3	68.8	69.4	67.5	66.2
5.	*Enterobacter* sp.	67.8	65.6	64.8	65.2	64.2
6.	*Alcaligenes* sp.	60.4	62.2	61.0	58.2	58.2
7.	*Escherichia* sp.	59.6	59.8	58.2	57.4	54.2
8.	*Micrococcus* sp.	55.4	56.4	55.2	54.0	52.3
9.	*Proteus* sp.	53.8	54.2	53.8	53.2	51.8
10.	*Staphylococcus* sp.	50.4	50.9	50.0	49.8	47.4
	SEd	3.15	2.85	2.87	2.88	2.93
	CD (P = 0.05)	6.32	2.72	5.76	5.76	5.88

4.6. SPECIES LEVEL IDENTIFICATION OF BACTERIAL ISOLATES BY 16S rRNA SEQUENCING

The bacterial isolates which were identified in genus level were subjected to Phylogenetic analysis by 16S rRNA sequencing and identified in species level. The bacteria *Bacillus* sp. was confirmed as was confirmed as *Bacillus subtilis* and *Serratia* sp. was confirmed as *Serratia marcescens*, *Pseudomonas* sp. was confirmed as *Pseudomonas fluorescens*. The Phylogenetic tree of the 16S rRNA sequences of three bacterial isolates was given in Fig – 2.

Fig: 2- Phylogenetic tree of the 16S rRNA sequences of three bacterial isolates

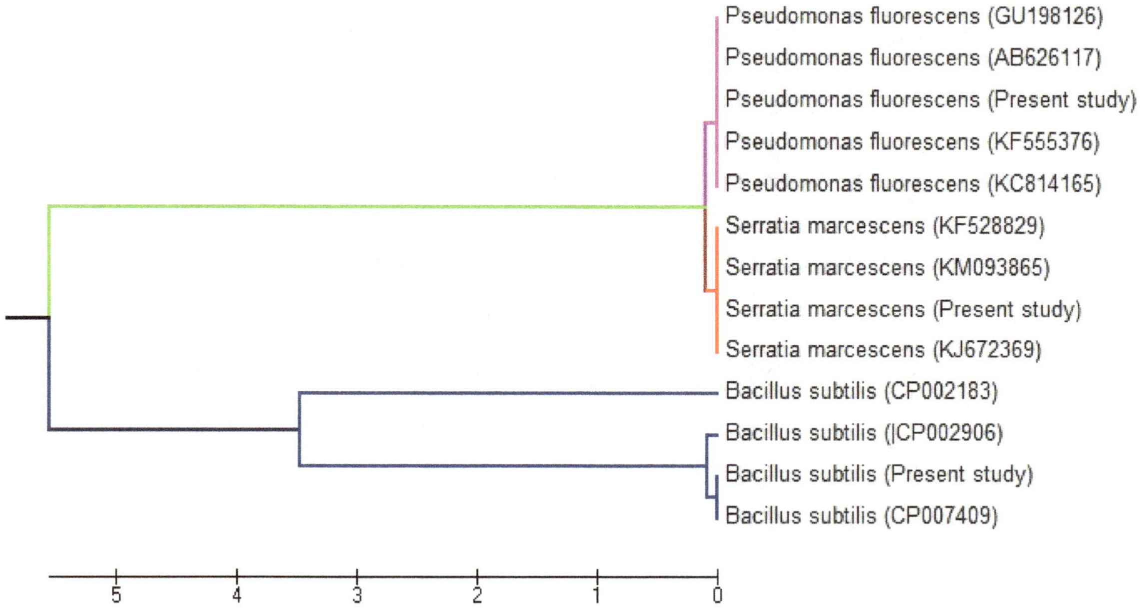

4.7. OPTIMIZATION FOR HEAVY METAL REMOVAL BY BACTERIAL ISOLATES

Among the three bioremediation studies (Bioaccumulation, Biosorption and Immobilization), immobilization study was more efficient in enhancing the heavy metal adsorption by the bacterial isolates. The three different efficient bacterial isolates (*Bacillus subtilis*, *Serratia marcescens* and *Pseudomonas fluorescens*) were considered for optimization study individually and as consortium because of their maximum bioremediation of heavy metals (Cr^{2+}, Zn^{2+}, Ni^{2+}, Cu^{2+} and Pb^{2+}).

4.7.1. Effect of pH on immobilization of heavy metals

The effect of pH (6, 7 and 8) on heavy metals (Cr^{2+}, Zn^{2+}, Ni^{2+}, Cu^{2+} and Pb^{2+}) adsorption by the immobilized bacterial strains was investigated and the results are listed in Table – 10. The maximum uptake of heavy metal took place at pH 7 by the bacterial consortium (*Bacillus subtilis* + *Serratia marcescens* + *Pseudomonas fluorescens*) with an adsorption level of 95.8 mg/L for Cr^{2+}, 95.4 mg/L for Zn^{2+}, 94.8 mg/L for Ni^{2+}, 93.2 mg/L for Cu^{2+} and 91.6 mg/L for Pb^{2+} respectively followed by *Bacillus subtilis* (88.7 mg/L for Cr^{2+}, 85.4 mg/L for Zn^{2+}, 85.1 mg/L for Ni^{2+}, 84.8 mg/L for Cu^{2+} and 83.2 mg/L for Pb^{2+}) and *Serratia marcescens* (82.6 mg/L for Cr^{2+}, 82.2 mg/L for Zn^{2+}, 81.8 mg/L for Ni^{2+}, 81.7 mg/L for Cu^{2+} and 80.6 mg/L for Pb^{2+}) as individual isolates. The minimum uptake of heavy metals was observed in *Pseudomonas fluorescens* with an adsorption level 78.5 mg/L for Cr^{2+}, 75.6 mg/L for Zn^{2+}, 75.4 mg/L for Ni^{2+}, 75.1 mg/L for Cu^{2+} and 74.3 mg/L for Pb^{2+}.

4.7.2 Effect of temperature on immobilization of heavy metals

The results of the effect of temperature (25°C, 30°C and 40°C) on heavy metals (Cr^{2+}, Zn^{2+}, Ni^{2+}, Cu^{2+} and Pb^{2+})adsorption was presented in Table – 11. The maximum uptake of heavy metals took place at the temperature of 30°C by the microbial consortium (*Bacillus subtilis* + *Serratia marcescens* + *Pseudomonas fluorescens*) with the adsorption level of (96.2 mg/L for Cr^{2+}, 95.3 mg/L for Zn^{2+}, 94.8 mg/L for Ni^{2+}, 92.4 mg/L for Cu^{2+} and 90.2 mg/L for Pb^{2+}) followed by *Bacillus subtilis* (88.2 mg/L for Cr^{2+}, 87.5 mg/L for Zn^{2+}, 86.5 mg/L for Ni^{2+}, 86.2 mg/L for Cu^{2+} and 85.8 mg/L for Pb^{2+}), *Serratia marcescens* (86.8 mg/L for Cr^{2+}, 85.4 mg/L for Zn^{2+}, 84.0 mg/L for Ni^{2+}, 80.4 mg/L for Cu^{2+} and 79.4 mg/L for Pb^{2+}) as individual isolates. The minimum uptake of heavy metals was observed in *Pseudomonas fluorescens* with an adsorption level 84.6 mg/L for Cr^{2+}, 83.2 mg/L for Zn^{2+}, 80.2 mg/L for Ni^{2+}, 79.2 mg/L for Cu^{2+} and 78.2 mg/L for Pb^{2+}. Next to 30°C, heavy metal removal was maximum in 40°C and least heavy metal removal was recorded at 25°C.

Table - 10: Effect of pH on immobilization of heavy metals

S. No.	Bacterial isolates	pH	Heavy metal adsorbed (Initial concentration – 100 mg/L)				
			Cr(VI)	Zn(II)	Ni(II)	Cu(II)	Pb(II)
1.	*Bacillus subtilis*	6	69.6	68.4	67.3	67.4	67.1
2.	*Serratia marcescens*		68.5	65.6	64.6	63.2	61.0
3.	*Pseudomonas fluorescens*		65.4	63.2	62.6	62.4	59.8
4.	Consortium (BS+SM+PF)		77.4	75.8	74.8	73.6	72.8
1.	*Bacillus subtilis*	7	88.7	85.4	85.1	84.8	83.2
2.	*Serratia marcescens*		82.6	82.2	81.8	81.7	80.6
3.	*Pseudomonas fluorescens*		78.5	75.6	75.4	75.1	74.3
4.	Consortium (BS+SM+PF)		95.8	95.4	94.8	93.2	91.6
1.	*Bacillus subtilis*	8	78.8	76.8	75.4	72.3	70.8
2.	*Serratia marcescens*		76.4	76.2	72.8	70.4	69.7
3.	*Pseudomonas fluorescens*		74.3	73.4	69.4	69.4	68.8
4.	Consortium (BS+SM+PF)		82.8	81.6	80.2	79.8	79.2
SEd			2.48	2.56	2.64	2.62	2.65
CD (P= 0.05)			4.98	5.14	5.30	5.26	5.32

4.7.3 Effect of carbon sources on immobilization of heavy metals

The effect of carbon sources (Glucose, Sucrose, Maltose and Dextrose) on immobilization of heavy metals (Cr^{2+}, Zn^{2+}, Ni^{2+}, Cu^{2+} and Pb^{2+}) was analyzed and the results were showed in Table – 12. The effect of carbon source on the heavy metals adsorption by individual (*Bacillus subtilis*, *Serratia marcescens* and *Pseudomonas fluorescens*) and consortium (*Bacillus subtilis* + *Serratia marcescens* + *Pseudomonas fluorescens*) of bacteria revealed that the adsorption of heavy metals were higher in the presence of dextrose than other sources of carbon. Further, it was observed that the highest adsorption of heavy metals was obtained in the case of bacterial consortia (89.6 mg/L for Cr^{2+}, 88.4 mg/L for Zn^{2+}, 85.8 mg/L for Ni^{2+}, 83.8 mg/L for Cu^{2+} and 80.8 mg/L for Pb^{2+}) followed by *Bacillus subtilis* (78.8 mg/L for Cr^{2+}, 75.2 mg/L for Zn^{2+}, 75.8 mg/L for Ni^{2+}, 74.2 mg/L for Cu^{2+} and 74.6 mg/L for Pb^{2+}), *Serratia marcescens* (76.4 mg/L for Cr^{2+}, 75.2 mg/L for Zn^{2+}, 74.5 mg/L for Ni^{2+}, 73.4 mg/L for Cu^{2+} and 72.8 mg/L for Pb^{2+}) and *Pseudomonas fluorescens* (74.8 mg/L for Cr^{2+}, 72.3 mg/L for Zn^{2+}, 72.1 mg/L for Ni^{2+}, 70.8 mg/L for Cu^{2+} and 70.2 mg/L for Pb^{2+}) with sucrose as a sole source of carbon followed by sucrose, maltose and glucose in the decreasing order of merit.

4.7.4 Effect of nitrogen sources on immobilization of heavy metals

The effect of nitrogen sources (Peptone, Yeast extract, Ammonium nitrate and Ammonium chloride) on immobilization of heavy metals was analyzed and the results were showed in Table – 13. The studies on the effect of nitrogen source on heavy metal (Cr^{2+}, Zn^{2+}, Ni^{2+}, Cu^{2+} and Pb^{2+}) adsorption revealed that the heavy metal adsorption by bacterial isolates was varied according to the nitrogen sources used. The maximum adsorption of heavy metals (89.2 mg/L for Cr^{2+}, 88.4 mg/L for Zn^{2+}, 87.2 mg/L for Ni^{2+}, 86.8 mg/L for Cu^{2+} and 84.4 mg/L for Pb^{2+}) was recorded by the bacterial consortia (*Bacillus subtilis* + *Serratia marcescens* + *Pseudomonas fluorescens*) followed by *Bacillus subtilis* (82.4 mg/L for Cr^{2+}, 80.8 mg/L for Zn^{2+}, 79.2 mg/L for Ni^{2+}, 78.4 mg/L for Cu^{2+} and 78.0 mg/L for Pb^{2+}), *Serratia marcescens* (81.6. mg/L for Cr^{2+}, 80.2 mg/L for Zn^{2+}, 77.4 mg/L for Ni^{2+}, 76.6 mg/L for Cu^{2+} and 76.2 mg/L for Pb^{2+}) and

Pseudomonas fluorescens (79.4 mg/L for Cr^{2+}, 78.0 mg/L for Zn^{2+}, 76.8 mg/L for Ni^{2+}, 74.3 mg/L for Cu^{2+} and 74.0 mg/L for Pb^{2+}) in the presence of ammonium nitrate as a nitrogen source. Next to ammonium nitrate, maximum heavy metal adsorption was observed in the presence of ammonium chloride and Yeast extract. The heavy metal adsorption was very low in the medium incorporated with peptone.

4.7.5. Effect of biomass concentration on immobilization of heavy metals

The effect of biomass concentration (2%, 3%, 4% and 5%) on immobilization of heavy metals (Cr^{2+}, Zn^{2+}, Ni^{2+}, Cu^{2+} and Pb^{2+}) was studied and the results were showed in Table – 14. The results showed that the adsorption of heavy metals by the bacterial isolates (*Bacillus subtilis*, *Serratia marcescens* and *Pseudomonas fluorescens*) individually and as consortium (*Bacillus subtilis* + *Serratia marcescens* + *Pseudomonas fluorescens*) varied according to the inoculum load. However, the highest heavy metal adsorption was recorded with 5% inoculum load of bacterial consortium (*Bacillus subtilis* + *Serratia marcescens* + *Pseudomonas fluorescens*) (86.6 mg/L for Cr^{2+}, 84.2 mg/L for Zn^{2+}, 81.6 mg/L for Ni^{2+}, 81.2 mg/L for Cu^{2+} and 80.7 mg/L for Pb^{2+}) followed by *Bacillus subtilis* (78.4 mg/L for Cr^{2+}, 75.3 mg/L for Zn^{2+}, 73.3 mg/L for Ni^{2+}, 72.4 mg/L for Cu^{2+} and 71.4 mg/L for Pb^{2+}), *Serratia marcescens* (74.1mg/L for Cr^{2+}, 72.6 mg/L for Zn^{2+}, 70.4 mg/L for Ni^{2+}, 69.8 mg/L for Cu^{2+} and 68.4 mg/L for Pb^{2+}) and *Pseudomonas fluorescens* (72.4 mg/L for Cr^{2+}, 71.8 mg/L for Zn^{2+}, 69.3 mg/L for Ni^{2+}, 68.5 mg/L for Cu^{2+} and 66.8 mg/L for Pb^{2+}). Next to 5% biomass concentration, heavy metal adsorption was maximum in 4 per cent and 3 percent inoculum load. The heavy metal adsorption was very low at 2per cent inoculum load.

4.7.6. Effect of incubation period on immobilization of heavy metals

The effect of incubation time (12 hrs, 18 hrs, 24 hrs and 30 hrs) for the heavy metals Cr^{2+}, Zn^{2+}, Ni^{2+}, Cu^{2+} and Pb^{2+}) adsorption by immobilized bacterial strains was studied and the results are presented in Table – 15. All the bacterial isolates showed highest adsorption level at 30 hrs and the treatment with bacterial consortia (*Bacillus subtilis* + *Serratia marcescens* + *Pseudomonas fluorescens*) showed highest adsorption efficiency level (88.4 mg/L for Cr^{2+}, 86.8 mg/L for Zn^{2+}, 86.2 mg/L for Ni^{2+}, 85.8 mg/L for Cu^{2+} and 84.8 mg/L for Pb^{2+}) at 30 hrs followed by *Bacillus subtilis* (82.2 mg/L for Cr^{2+}, 80.4 mg/L for Zn^{2+}, 79.7 mg/L for Ni^{2+}, 79.0 mg/L for Cu^{2+} and 77.6 mg/L for Pb^{2+}), *Serratia marcescens* (80.1 mg/L for Cr^{2+}, 79.4 mg/L for Zn^{2+}, 79.1 mg/L for Ni^{2+}, 77.7 mg/L for Cu^{2+} and 76.7 mg/L for Pb^{2+}) and *Pseudomonas fluorescens* (79.8 mg/L for Cr^{2+}, 77.6 mg/L for Zn^{2+}, 76.5 mg/L for Cu^{2+}, 73.2 mg/L for Cu^{2+} and 71.0 mg/L for Pb^{2+}) as individual isolates. Overall, it was concluded that pH 7, temperature of 30°C, dextrose as the carbon source, ammonium nitrate as nitrogen source, 5% inoculum load and 30 hrs of incubation time were found as optimum for the treatment with bacterial consortium (*Bacillus subtilis* + *Serratia marcescens* + *Pseudomonas fluorescens*) to be more efficient as compared to individual isolates and record the maximum adsorption of the heavy metals (Cr^{2+}, Zn^{2+}, Ni^{2+}, Cu^{2+} and Pb^{2+}).

4.8. SURVIVAL OF INDIVIDUAL BACTERIAL ISOLATES AND CONSORTIUM IN ALGINATE BEADS

Alginate beads supported the required population levels of bacterial isolates upto six months. The population of the microbes was increased in both consortium and single inoculants packets during the first month of storage and thereafter reduced with increase in the period of storage upto six months. The surviving populations were 74.06×10^8 cfu g^{-1} for *Bacillus subtilis*, 62.55×10^8 cfu g^{-1} for *Serratia marcescens*, and 60.84×10^8 cfu g^{-1} for *Pseudomonas fluorescens* in single inoculants preparation at initial stage of storage. The surviving population was 76.08×10^8 cfu g^{-1} in bacterial consortium (*Bacillus subtilis* + *Serratia marcescens* + *Pseudomonas fluorescens*) at initial stage of storage. However, it was found that the required inoculants cell load was maintained upto six months. The surviving populations in the sixth month were 63.38×10^8 cfu g^{-1} for *Bacillus subtilis*, 57.01×10^8 cfu g^{-1} for *Serratia marcescens*, 56.81×10^8 cfu g^{-1} for *Pseudomonas fluorescens* in single inoculants preparation and 64.62×10^8 cfu g^{-1} in consortium (Table – 16).

4.9. PHYSICO - CHEMICAL PROPERTIES OF BIOREMEDIATED TANNERY EFFLUENT USING IMMOBILIZED (ALGINATE BEADS) BACTERIAL CONSORTIUM

The physico - chemical parameters of the (immobilized bacterial consortium *Bacillus subtilis + Serratia marcescens + Pseudomonas fluorescens*) bioremediated effluent *viz.*, colour, BOD, COD, Total nitrogen, Nitrate, Heavy metals, Sodium, Potassium were estimated. (Table - 17). The colour of the bioremediated tannery effluent sample was found to be light brown to colourless and was also odorless. The temperature of treated tannery effluent was 30°C in the sixth month. The pH of the treated Tannery effluent was neutral. The TSS present in bioremediated Tannery effluent was 95 mg/L and TDS were 108 mg/L in the sixth month. The BOD and COD were varied within a span of six months to 220 mg/L and 26 mg/L respectively. The concentration of heavy metals was found highly decreased in sixth month (Chromium 0.1 mg/L, Zinc 0.2 mg/L, Nickel o.3 mg/L, Copper 0.1 mg/ L and Lead 0.5 mg/ L).

Table - 11: Effect of temperature on immobilization of heavy metals

S. No.	Bacterial isolates	Temperature	Heavy metal adsorbed (mg/L) (Initial concentration – 100 mg/L)				
			Cr(VI)	Zn(II)	Ni(II)	Cu(II)	Pb(II)
1.	*Bacillus subtilis*	25°C	70.2	70.6	70.2	69.8	67.4
2.	*Serratia marcescens*		68.4	68.2	66.4	68.8	60.2
3.	*Pseudomonas fluorescens*		64.8	64.2	58.5	60.2	56.2
4.	Consortium (BS+SM+PF)		78.2	77.4	76.8	75.4	73.8
1.	*Bacillus subtilis*	30°C	88.2	87.5	86.5	86.2	85.8
2.	*Serratia marcescens*		86.8	85.4	84.0	80.4	79.4
3.	*Pseudomonas fluorescens*		84.6	83.2	80.2	79.2	78.2
4.	Consortium (BS+SM+PF)		96.2	95.3	94.8	92.4	90.2
1.	*Bacillus subtilis*	40°C	82.8	78.6	76.7	75.8	72.8
2.	*Serratia marcescens*		80.8	78.0	74.2	72.4	70.2
3.	*Pseudomonas fluorescens*		76.4	76.8	70.8	70.8	68.8
4.	Consortium (BS+SM+PF)		88.4	86.8	84.8	82.2	80.5
Sed			2.68	2.56	2.85	2.49	2.86
CD (P= 0.05)			5.38	5.14	5.71	4.99	5.74

Table – 12: Effect of carbon sources on immobilization of heavy metals

S. No.	Bacterial isolates	Carbon sources	Heavy metal adsorbed (mg/L) (Initial concentration – 100 mg/L)				
			Cr(VI)	Zn(II)	Ni(II)	Cu(II)	Pb(II)
1.	*Bacillus subtilis*	Glucose	49.6	49.4	48.8	48.2	46.4
2.	*Serratia marcescens*		47.5	46.4	45.8	44.1	45.6
3.	*Pseudomonas fluorescens*		43.2	43.6	40.3	39.2	40.2
4.	Consortium (BS+SM+PF)		56.8	54.8	53.4	51.8	52.2
1.	*Bacillus subtilis*	Sucrose	69.6	68.2	66.4	65.8	63.2
2.	*Serratia marcescens*		68.4	64.8	63.8	62.1	60.8
3.	*Pseudomonas fluorescens*		64.3	62.3	60.2	60.0	58.2
4.	Consortium (BS+SM+PF)		78.4	76.5	74.8	72.2	69.8
1.	*Bacillus subtilis*	Maltose	58.7	56.2	54.8	52.8	52.2
2.	*Serratia marcescens*		55.2	53.8	52.2	51.2	50.1
3.	*Pseudomonas fluorescens*		52.8	50.8	51.5	49.8	48.6
4.	Consortium (BS+SM+PF)		69.4	77.4	67.4	64.3	62.3
1.	*Bacillus subtilis*	Dextrose	78.8	75.2	75.8	74.2	74.6
2.	*Serratia marcescens*		76.4	75.2	74.5	73.4	72.8
3.	*Pseudomonas fluorescens*		74.8	72.3	72.1	70.8	70.2
4.	Consortium (BS+SM+PF)		89.6	88.4	85.8	83.8	80.8
SEd			3.30	3.31	3.20	3.15	2.99
CD (P= 0.05)			6.62	6.64	6.42	6.32	6.00

Table - 13: Effect of nitrogen sources on immobilization of heavy metals

S. No.	Bacterial isolates	Nitrogen sources	Heavy metal adsorbed (mg/L) (Initial concentration – 100 mg/L)				
			Cr(VI)	Zn(II)	Ni(II)	Cu(II)	Pb(II)
1.	*Bacillus subtilis*	Peptone	54.5	53.8	52.4	52.2	50.6
2.	*Serratia marcescens*		52.8	51.7	50.8	50.2	49.6
3.	*Pseudomonas fluorescens*		51.1	50.2	51.4	49.4	48.8
4.	Consortium (BS+SM+PF)		68.4	67.8	66.2	64.4	60.8
1.	*Bacillus subtilis*	Yeast extract	66.6	66.2	65.8	64.7	64.3
2.	*Serratia marcescens*		65.8	64.4	64.0	63.7	62.5
3.	*Pseudomonas fluorescens*		63.8	62.4	62.2	61.5	60.2
4.	Consortium (BS+SM+PF)		76.8	76.8	76.2	75.4	74.8
1.	*Bacillus subtilis*	Ammonium nitrate	82.4	80.8	79.2	78.4	78.0
2.	*Serratia marcescens*		81.6	80.2	77.4	76.6	76.2
3.	*Pseudomonas fluorescens*		79.4	78.0	76.8	74.3	74.0
4.	Consortium (BS+SM+PF)		89.2	88.4	87.2	86.8	84.4
1.	*Bacillus subtilis*	Ammonium chloride	75.2	74.8	73.2	71.4	68.2
2.	*Serratia marcescens*		72.4	72.2	70.4	69.9	67.4
3.	*Pseudomonas fluorescens*		71.8	71.0	69.8	68.5	65.6
4.	Consortium (BS+SM+PF)		82.8	82.2	80.8	79.8	79.2
Sed			2.84	2.85	2.73	2.72	2.73
CD (P= 0.05)			5.69	5.72	5.48	5.45	5.48

Table - 14: Effect of biomass concentration on immobilization of heavy metals

S. No.	Bacterial isolates	Biomass conc.	Heavy metal adsorbed (mg/L) (Initial concentration – 100 mg/L)				
			Cr(VI)	Zn(II)	Ni(II)	Cu(II)	Pb(II)
1.	*Bacillus subtilis*	2%	54.2	50.7	49.8	49.3	48.2
2.	*Serratia marcescens*		50.8	49.4	47.2	46.5	44.8
3.	*Pseudomonas fluorescens*		48.2	46.8	44.6	42.8	39.8
4.	Consortium (BS+SM+PF)		64.8	62.8	59.4	56.4	55.9
1.	*Bacillus subtilis*	3%	65.4	64.2	62.1	60.8	59.4
2.	*Serratia marcescens*		62.2	60.8	60.2	56.2	54.6
3.	*Pseudomonas fluorescens*		61.8	58.5	54.4	50.4	49.7
4.	Consortium (BS+SM+PF)		76.4	74.2	70.6	69.8	68.7
1.	*Bacillus subtilis*	4%	68.2	66.8	65.8	63.8	64.4
2.	*Serratia marcescens*		66.1	64.2	62.2	60.2	59.7
3.	*Pseudomonas fluorescens*		64.3	60.7	58.4	56.6	54.8
4.	Consortium (BS+SM+PF)		80.8	78.2	76.4	72.9	72.2
1.	*Bacillus subtilis*	5%	78.4	75.3	73.3	72.4	71.4
2.	*Serratia marcescens*		74.1	72.6	70.4	69.8	68.4
3.	*Pseudomonas fluorescens*		72.4	71.8	69.3	68.5	66.8
4.	Consortium (BS+SM+PF)		86.6	84.2	81.6	81.2	80.7
Sed			2.67	2.66	2.63	2.70	2.79
CD (P= 0.05)			5.35	5.34	5.28	5.42	5.60

Table - 15: Effect of incubation period on immobilization of heavy metals

S. No.	Bacterial isolates	Incubation hours	Heavy metal adsorbed (mg/L) (Initial concentration – 100 mg/L)				
			Cr(VI)	Zn(II)	Ni(II)	Cu(II)	Pb(II)
1.	*Bacillus subtilis*	12 hrs	55.4	53.2	51.8	50.4	49.8
2.	*Serratia marcescens*		52.3	50.4	49.2	47.6	44.6
3.	*Pseudomonas fluorescens*		50.7	42.6	42.8	44.8	39.6
4.	Consortium (BS+SM+PF)		64.6	62.8	60.2	58.2	54.4
1.	*Bacillus subtilis*	18 hrs	66.2	63.8	62.4	62.8	61.4
2.	*Serratia marcescens*		63.4	61.4	61.1	58.7	58.2
3.	*Pseudomonas fluorescens*		61.8	60.7	58.8	58.6	56.7
4.	Consortium (BS+SM+PF)		73.8	73.2	72.7	70.8	70.2
1.	*Bacillus subtilis*	24 hrs	76.8	76.2	75.4	73.4	70.1
2.	*Serratia marcescens*		74.2	73.3	72.6	70.4	69.8
3.	*Pseudomonas fluorescens*		70.6	70.2	69.4	68.7	68.2
4.	Consortium (BS+SM+PF)		81.2	80.1	79.8	79.4	78.8
1.	*Bacillus subtilis*	30 hrs	82.2	80.4	79.7	79.0	77.6
2.	*Serratia marcescens*		80.1	79.4	79.1	77.7	76.7
3.	*Pseudomonas fluorescens*		79.8	77.6	76.5	73.2	71.0
4.	Consortium (BS+SM+PF)		88.4	86.8	86.2	85.8	84.8
Sed			2.84	3.10	3.14	3.05	3.24
CD (P= 0.05)			5.70	6.22	6.30	6.12	6.50

Table - 16: Survival of individual and consortium in alginate beads

Storage period in months	Number of cfu × 10^8 g^{-1} Alginate beads			
	Bacillus subtilis (BS)	*Serratia marcescens* (SM)	*Pseudomonas fluorescens* (PF)	Bacterial consortium (BS+SM+PF)
0	74.06	62.55	60.84	76.08
1	73.24	63.18	62.11	78.84
2	72.8	62.40	61.21	76.01
3	70.21	60.34	60.32	71.04
4	67.42	59.03	58.00	69.57
5	66.89	58.61	57.23	67.64
6	63.38	57.01	56.81	64.62

Values in parenthesis are $\log_{10}$ transformed values

Table - 17: Physiochemical properties of bioremediated tannery effluent using immobilized (Alginate beads) bacterial consortium

Parameters	Raw Effluent	Bioremediated effluent
Colour	Brown	Light brown
Odour	Offensive	Odourless
Temperature	38°C	30°C
pH	9.7	7.2
Electrical conductivity (dsm^{-1})	30.2	11.8
Total hardness (mg/L)	5200	66
Total suspended solids (mg/L)	316	95
Total dissolved solids (mg/L)	1500	108
Biological Oxygen Demand (mg/L)	1280	220
Chemical Oxygen Demand (mg/L)	2037	26
Carbonate (mg/L)	860	52
Bicarbonate (mg/L)	1428	74
Calcium (mg/L)	160	72
Magnesium (mg/L)	57	22
Chloride (mg/L)	1464	99
Sodium (mg/L)	188	14
Potassium (mg/L)	603	72
Fluoride (mg/L)	6.0	2.2
Nitrate (mg/L)	45	14.8
Nitrite (mg/L)	33	27
Sulphate (mg/L)	349	96
Chromium (mg/L)	146	0.1
Nickel (mg/L)	57	0.3
Zinc (mg/L)	36	0.2
Copper (mg/L)	29	0.1
Iron (mg/L)	19	0.0
Cadminum (mg/L)	5.4	0.2
Lead (mg/L)	4.6	0.5
Manganese (mg/L)	9.9	0.2

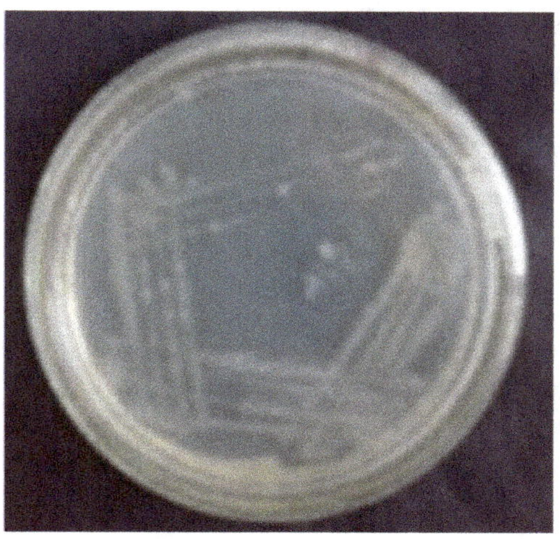

PLATE – 1: *Bacillus subtilis* on Nutrient agar

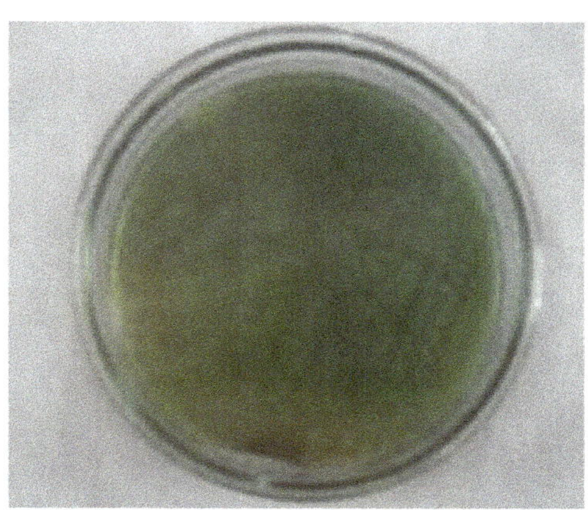

PLATE – 2: *Pseudomonas fluorescens* on Nutrient agar

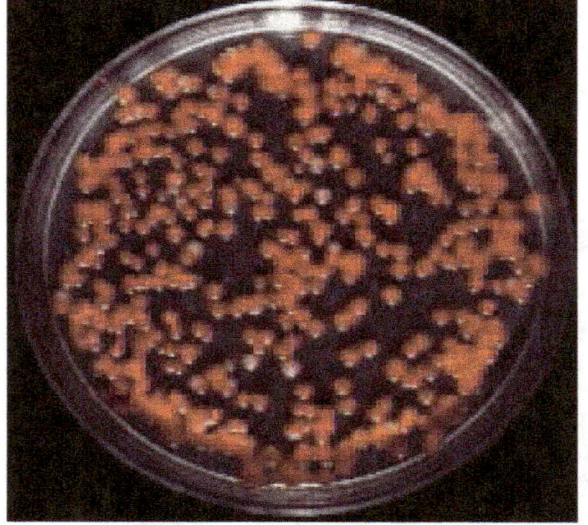

PLATE – 3: *Serratia marcescens* on Nutrient agar

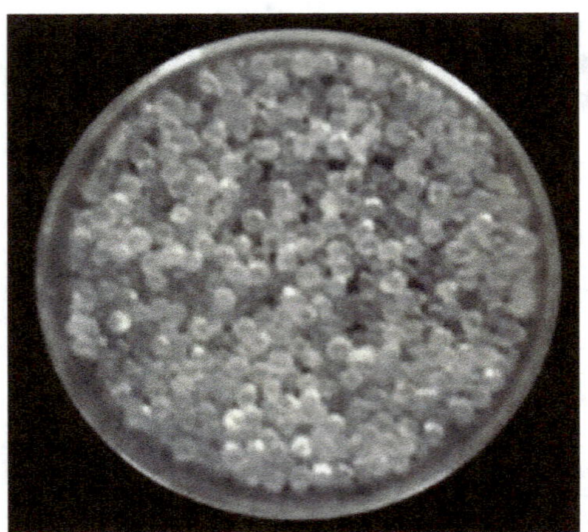

PLATE – 4: Bacterial Consortium in Immobilized Beads

PLATE – 5: Untreated tannery effluent

PLATE – 6: Bioremediated Tannery effluent

5. DISCUSSION

5.1. ANALYSIS OF PHYSICO – CHEMICAL AND BIOLOGICAL CHARACTERESTICS OF TANNERY EFFLUENT

Tanneries are typically characterized as pollution intensive industrial complexes which generates widely varying high strength waste waters (Saranraj *et al.*, 2010). Tanning industry also has one of the highest toxic intensity/unit of output (Khan *et al.*, 2006). Tannery effluent was reported to cause adverse effect on plant growth (Vereheijen *et al.*, 1996; Thirunavukarasu and Lourdraj, 2005). With all the river basins having deficit volume of water for irrigation, the effluent from industries can reduces the pressure on water scarcity for irrigation as well as the effluents contaminated the water bodies increased the water scarcity (Sadeeshkumar *et al.*, 2012).

Tannery effluents which exhibit very high value for chromium, sulphide, and chloride, TDS, TSS, BOD and COD in the water stream or land, discharged into water bodies and have adverse impact on aquatic life and severely affect the mitotic process and reduces seed germination in extensively cultivated pulse crops (Altaf, 2008). Thus, the impact of leather tanning industry on the environment is ongoing and increasing the problem and hence, need to develop the eco-friendly methods to treat the waste water from tannery industry (Belay, 2010).

In the present study, physico - chemical characteristics of the collected tannery effluent was analyzed. The tannery effluent was acidic in nature, brown coloured and emitted unpleasant smell. The temperature of collected tannery effluent was 38°C, electrical conductivity (EC) was 30.2 dSm^{-1} and hardness was 5200 mg/L. The TSS and TDS present in collected tannery effluent were 316 mg/L and 1500 mg/L respectively. It also showed high BOD (1280 mg/L) and COD (2037 mg/L). High amount of chloride (1464 mg/L), Calcium (160 mg/L), magnesium (57 mg/L), sodium (188 mg/L), potassium (603 mg/L), fluoride (6.0 mg/L), nitrate (45 mg/L), nitrite (33 mg/L), sulphate (349 mg/L) and the toxic heavy metals (Cr^{2+}-146, Ni^{2+}-57, Zn^{2+}- 36 mg/L, Cu^{2+}- 29 mg/L, Fe^{2+}- 19.00 mg/ L, Cd^{2+}- 5.4 mg/L, Pb^{2+}- 4.6 mg/L, and Mn^{2+}- 9.9 mg/L) were recorded in the collected tannery effluent sample.

The finding of the present study was similar with the findings reported by Singh and Bhatti (2005); Sahu *et al.* (2007); Mythili and Karthikeyan (2011). The alkaline nature of sewage water may be due to presence of Ca and Mg ions in high concentrations. The colour of the effluent might be due to the presence of biodegradable and non-degradable high molecular weight organic compounds and high amount of inorganic chemicals like sodium and chromium used during the processing and the odour may be due to putrefaction of the organic residues from the processed skin and hides (Smrithi and Usha, 2012). The presence of higher level of total suspended solids (TSS) and total dissolved solids (TDS) in the effluent might be due to presence of insoluble organic matter from the animal skin and unused inorganic salts used for tanning (Nagarajan *et al.*, 2005; Mythili and Kerthikeyan, 2011). The BOD and organic carbon were higher in the untreated water indicating the presence of high content of organic matter (Pragati Saline and Ajay Kumar, 2012). The record of high COD might be due to presence of oxidizable organic matter from the animal skin (Tesena *et al.* 2002; Ravi Babu *et al.*, 2007; Saranraj *et al.,* 2012).

In addition, the soil samples collected from the agricultural land irrigated with tannery effluent had high level of several toxic metals as copper, zinc, lead, manganese and iron. It indicated that the selected effluent used to irrigate agricultural land was not fit for agricultural practices as high metal content may directly or indirectly interfere with the metabolic activities of crop plants by altering the conformation of proteins, for example enzymes, transporters or regulators (Sharma *et al.*, 2004; Bhalli and Quiser, 2006).

5.2. SCREENING OF BACTERIAL ISOLATES FOR ITS HEAVY METAL RESISTANCE

Bioremediation is an emerging modern technology in which the removal of harmful environmental pollutants is practiced using living organisms including microbes and plants. Heavy metals are non-biodegradable and persist for longer periods in aquatic as well as terrestrial environments (Widdel *al et.*, 2006). Heavy metals containing waste water can exert detrimental effect on human health and environment due to the toxicity of heavy metals. In order to remove the metals from industrial effluents, many attempts related to heavy metal remediation have been carried out all around the world. However, high investment and operating cost of some complicated physico- chemical processes have limited these efforts in under developed countries (Al- Enezi 2004).

In the present research, ten different bacterial isolates were identified by staining techniques, motility test, platting on selective medium and biochemical tests. The identified bacterial isolates were *Pseudomonas* sp. (P1), *Proteus* sp., *Bacillus* sp., *Escherichia* sp., *Serratia* sp., *Pseudomonas* sp. (P2), *Staphylococcus* sp., *Enterobacter* sp., *Alcaligenes* sp. and *Micrococcus* sp.

In the present research, the heavy metal resistance of bacterial isolates which were isolated from the tannery effluent was screened against toxic heavy metals by disc diffusion method. Among the ten bacterial isolates tested, all the isolates (*Pseudomonas* sp. (P1), *Proteus* sp., *Bacillus* sp., *Escherichia* sp., *Serratia* sp., *Pseudomonas* sp. (P2), *Staphylococcus* sp., *Enterobacter* sp., *Alcaligenes* sp. and *Micrococcus* sp.) were resistant to all the heavy metals.

Metal resistance reflects the ability of an organism to survive in environment with high concentration of metals or to accumulate high concentration of metals (Azza *et al.*, 2009). The heavy metal resistance mechanisms take several forms including transformation of toxic metals resulting in the release of metal ions (Williams *et al.*, 2011). Heavy metal ions might also be detoxified by inducible ions efflux system that reduces the extracellular concentrations of the given heavy metal by active export of the bacterial cell which could mediate biochemical reactions such as precipitation of heavy metals with CO_2 during growth.

Metal resistance determinants were initially found on bacterial plasmids. *Escherichia coli* and *Alcaligenes* have possession of a heavy metal resistance. Microbes may play a large role in the biogeochemical cycling of toxic heavy metals also in cleaning up or remediating metal-contaminated environments. There is also evidence of a correlation between tolerance to heavy metals and antibiotic resistance, a global problem currently threatening the treatment of infections in plants, animals, and humans. To survive under metal-stressed conditions, bacteria have evolved several types of mechanisms to tolerate the uptake of heavy metal ions. These mechanisms include the efflux of metal ions outside the cell, accumulation and complexation of the metal ions inside the cell, and reduction of the heavy metal ions to a less toxic state (Nies, 2003; Anne Spain *et al.*, 2003).

Karami and Shamsuddin (2010) reported that the highest incidence of the biochemical activity of isolates and metal resistance was recorded by phosphate solubilizers with Cr, Zn and Pb. This implies that phosphate solubilization is not the only mechanism adopted by bacteria towards metals in soil but that siderophores and acid production are also involved in mobilizing metals.

Amalesh Samanta *et al.* (2012) explained that the *Bacillus subtilis* was able to interact with a range of toxic metals, including copper, iron, magnesium, gold and lead. This ability was attributed to differences between the net negative charge of bacteria and the cationic charge of many metals. The theory stated that nucleation sites on the cell surface had the ability to bind metals of opposite charge. Once bound to the cell wall, this resulted in a nucleation site where a large concentration of metals could bind and precipitate on the cell wall.

5.3. BIOREMEDIATION OF HEAVY METALS USING BACTERIAL ISOLATES

The bioremediation of heavy metals using microorganisms has received a great deal of attention in recent years, not only as a scientific novelty but also for its potential application in industry. Metal accumulative bioprocess generally falls into one of two categories, bisorptive uptake by non-living, non - growing biomass or biomass products and bioaccumulation by living cells (Doenmez and Aksu, 2001; Lone *et al.*, 2008).

Microorganisms play a significant role in bioremediation of heavy metal contaminated soil and wastewater. Many microorganisms like fungi, bacteria and microalgae have been recognized for their ability to either resist the toxic effect of heavy metals so that the heavy metal ions become less toxic or non toxic to them (Ilhan *et al.*, 2004). Thus, bioremediation of heavy metals aims at sequestering the metals to make them unavailable to flow in the ecosystem, or extract to mobilizing them for reuse or safe disposal (Crawford 1983). The properties of microorganisms to adsorb and bioaccumulate heavy metals give potential for cheap alternative method of heavy metal removal from industrial wastewaters. Both living and dead biomaterials are capable of removing heavy metal ions from wastewater through diverse mechanisms collectively known as biosorption (Abou Shanab *et al.,* 2008).

In the present study, heavy metal adsorption by living bacterial cells isolated from tannery effluent was studied. The bioaccumulation studies revealed that the highest heavy metals adsorption was showed by the bacteria *Bacillus* sp. (58.5 mg/L for Cr^{2+}, 58.1 mg/L for Zn^{2+}, 57.3 mg/L for Ni^{2+}, 57.8 mg/L for Cu^{2+} and 54.2 mg/L for Pb^{2+}) followed by *Serratia* sp., *Pseudomonas* sp. (P1), *Pseudomona* sp. (P2), *Enterobacte* sp., *Escherichia* sp., *Alcaligenes* sp., *Micrococcus* sp., and *Proteus* sp. whereas *Staphylococcus* sp. showed the lowest activity of heavy metal adsorption (33.2 mg/L for Cr^{2+}, 33.0 mg/L for Zn^{2+}, 32.6 mg/L for Ni^{2+}, 32.8 mg/L for Cu^{2+} and 30.4 mg/L for Pb^{2+}).

Removal of heavy metals from contaminated domestic industrial effluent using eight resistant indigenous bacteria isolated from acclimatized activated sludge was investigated. Molecular identification using 16S rDNA amplification revealed that all strains were Gram negative among which two were resistant to each of copper, cadmium and cobalt while one was resistant to each of chromium and the heavy metal mixture. They were identified as *Enterobacter* sp. (Cu1), *Enterobacter* sp. (Cu2), *Stenotrophomonas* sp. (Cd1), *Providencia* sp. (Cd2), *Chryseobacterium* sp. (Co1), *Comamonas* sp. (Co2), *Ochrobactrum* sp. (Cr) and *Delftia* sp. (M1) according to their resistance pattern. Strains Cu1, Cd1, Co2 and Cr were able to resist 275 mg Cu/L, 320 mg Cd/L, 140 mg Co/L and 29 mg Cr/L respectively. The four resistant strains were used as a mixture to remove heavy metals (elevated concentrations) and reduce the organic load of wastewater effluent (Ebtesam *et al.*, 2013).

Microbes deals with poisonous chemicals by applying enzymes to convert one chemical into another form and taking energy or utilizable matter from this process. The chemical transformation generally involves the breaking of large molecules into several small molecules in simpler form. In view of the interest in water and wastewater treatment, the response of microorganisms towards toxic heavy metals is of importance. In some cases the by-products of microbial remediation are not only harmless but may prove useful (Gupta *et al.*, 2003).

The microbes live in the sludge of the treatment plants, digest the solids and breakdown of various compounds. As these microbes are living organisms, they require certain nutrients to survive in the environment. In the wastewater treatment system is a vast array of microbes present, that is aerobic, anaerobic and facultative, each performing specific functions in their respective parts of the system. Each of these microbial species has a tolerance of ecological minimums and maximums with regard to various conditions such as pH, temperature, dissolved oxygen levels and nutrient levels (Vatsouria *et al.*, 2005).

Uptake of metal by microbes can either occur actively (bioaccumulation) and/or passively (biosorption). Studies conducted in large-scale systems have shown that, biosorptive processes are more applicable than the bioaccumulative processes. This is because of living systems (active uptake) often require the addition of nutrients and hence, increases the biological oxygen demand or chemical oxygen demand in the effluent (Hussein *et al.*, 2005). Sharma *et al.* (2004) carried out the study and the results revealed that *Klebsiella pneumoniae* has potential to bioaccumulate heavy metals at high concentrations (15 mM).

Heavy metal adsorption by dead bacterial cells was investigated in the present study. Among the ten bacterial isolates which was isolated from tannery effluent, *Bacillus* sp. showed the maximum heavy metal adsorption (70.4 mg/L for Cr^{2+}, 69.6 mg/L for Zn^{2+}, 70.3 mg/L for Ni^{2+}, 68.9 mg/L for Cu^{2+} and 64.6 mg/L for Pb^{2+}) followed by *Serratias* sp., *Pseudomonas* sp. (P1), *Pseudomonas* sp. (P2), *Enterobacter* sp., *Escherichia* sp., *Alcaligenes* sp., *Micrococcus* sp. and *Proteus* sp. The bacterial isolate *Staphylococcus* sp. showed the minimum adsorption of the heavy metals (42.4 mg/L for Cr^{2+}, 43.5 mg/L for Zn^{2+}, 42.2 mg/L for Ni^{2+}, 40.8 mg/L for Cu^{2+} and 39.8 mg/L for Pb^{2+}).

Sahar Alzubaidy (2012) evaluated the resistance of *Serratia marcescens* obtained from soil and water to metals chlorides (Zn^{2+}, Hg^{2+}, Fe^{2+}, Al^{3+} and Pb^{2+}). Four isolates were identified as *Serratia marcescens* (S4) and selected for this study according to their resistance to five heavy metals. The ability of *Serratia marcescens* (S4) to grow in different concentrations of metals chloride (200 - 1200 µg/ml) was tested. The highest concentration that *Serratia marcescens* (S4) tolerate was 1000 µg/ml for Zn^{2+}, Hg^{2+}, Fe^{2+}, Al^{3+} and Pb^{2+} and 300 µg/ml for Hg^{+2} through 24 hrs incubation at 37°C. The isolates showed the ability to grow in different pH values (4, 7 and 9) in presence of four metals in all pH values (1000 µg/ml) and unability to grow with 300 µg/ml Hg^{2+}. The highest Zn^{2+} removal ratio was 75 per cent then Pb^{2+} 55 per cent while Fe^{2+} has the lowest removal ratio (48%).

In the present research, heavy metal adsorption by immobilized bacterial isolates were analyzed. Among the ten bacterial isolates, *Bacillus* sp. showed maximum heavy metal adsorption (79.2 mg/L for Cr^{2+}, 78.4 mg/L for Zn^{2+}, 77.4 mg/L for Ni^{2+}, 76.8 mg/L for Cu^{2+} and 74.2 mg/L for Pb^{2+}) followed by *Serratia* sp., *Pseudomonas* sp., *Pseudomonas* sp., *Enterobacter* sp., *Escherichia* sp., *Alcaligenes* sp., *Micrococcus* sp. and *Proteus* sp. While, Staphylococcus sp. showed the least heavy metal adsorption (50.4 mg/L for Cr^{2+}, 50.9 mg/L for Zn^{2+}, 50.0 mg/L for Ni^{2+}, 49.8 mg/L for Cu^{2+} and 47.4 mg/L for Pb^{2+}).

It was reported that the immobilized bacterial cells have greater adsorption capacity than that of dead or live cells because the bacterial cells consists of small particles with low density, poor mechanical strength and little rigidity in their cell surface (Leusch *et al.*, 2005). These results are also supported by other authors (Costa and Leite, 2000; Sudha and Abraham, 2003; Wei- Bin *et al.*, 2006; Vijayaraghavan and Yeoung - Sang, 2007).

Immobilized cells have been reported to be very effective in heavy metal removal. Heavy metal toxicity and other extreme properties of waste effluents that may limit the use of living cell systems Immobilized cells appear to be of greater potential in controlling particle size, better capability of regeneration, easy separation of biomass and effluent and recirculation, high biomass loading, minimal clogging and reduced depletion of nutrient source (Katiyar and Katiyar, 1997). It has also been reported that immobilized cells have found to be most effective in designing small and large scale bioreactors for heavy metal degradation (James, 2002).

Microorganisms play a vital role in heavy metal contaminated soil and wastewater by the mechanisms of biosorption. In this study, heavy metal resistant bacteria were isolated from an electroplating industrial effluent samples that uses copper, cadmium and lead for plating. These isolates were characterized to evaluate their applicability for heavy metal removal from industrial wastewaters. The physico -

chemical parameters of the samples were initially analyzed. The optimum conditions of pH, biomass concentration and heavy metal concentration were determined for the microbial growth on biosorbents and correlated with heavy metal removal. The observed optimum conditions were applied for the biosorption process carried out in immobilized and dead bacterial isolates. The biosorption of immobilized cells of *Bacillus* sp. was 69.34 per cent of copper, *Pseudomonas* sp. was 90.41per cent of cadmium and *Micrococcus* sp. was 84.27 per cent of lead, whereas the dead cells of *Bacillus* sp. was 44.73 per cent of copper, *Pseudomonas* sp. was 86.66 per cent of cadmium and *Micrococcus* sp. was 79.22 per cent. Experimental results revealed that all the immobilized isolates have potential application for the removal of copper, cadmium and lead from industrial wastewater than the dead bacterial cells (Johncy Rani *et al.*, 2010).

In this study, the remediation of tannery effluent carried out by three ways such as bioaccumulation (living bacterial cell), biosorption (dead bacterial cell) and immobilization (immobilized bacterial cells). The efficient bioremediation of heavy metals (Cr^{2+}, Zn^{2+}, Ni^{2+}, Cu^{2+} and Pb^{2+}) was recorded in immobilization when compared to bioaccumulation and biosorption.

The bacterial isolates which were identified in genus level were subjected to 16S rRNA sequencing and identified in species level. The bacteria *Proteus* sp. was confirmed as *Proteus mirabilis*, *Bacillus* sp. was confirmed as *Bacillus subtilis*, *Serratia* sp. was confirmed as *Serratia marcescens* and *Pseudomonas* sp. was confirmed as *Pseudomonas fluorescens*.

5.4. OPTIMIZATION FOR HEAVY METAL REMOVAL BY BACTERIAL ISOLATES

Optimization of bioremediation processes is a complex system of many factors. These factors include: the existence of a microbial population capable of degrading the pollutants (Tmoney *et al.*, 1987). In the present research, the effect of pH (6, 7 and 8), temperature (25°C, 30°C and 40°C), carbon sources (glucose, sucrose, maltose and dextrose), nitrogen sources (peptone, yeast extract, ammonium nitrate and ammonium chloride), biomass concentration (2%, 3%, 4% and 5%) and incubation hours (12 hrs, 18 hrs, 24 hrs and 30 hrs) on heavy metals adsorption by the immobilized bacterial strains was investigated. The maximum uptake of heavy metal took place by the bacterial consortium (*Bacillus subtilis* + *Serratia marcescens* + *Pseudomonas fluorescens*) followed by *Bacillus subtilis* and *Serratia marcescens* as individual isolates. The minimum uptake of heavy metals was observed in *Pseudomonas fluorescens*. Overall, it was concluded that the pH 7, temperature of 30°C, sucrose as the carbon source, ammonium nitrate as nitrogen source, 5 per cent inoculum load and 30 hrs of incubation time were found as optimum for the treatment with bacterial consortium to be more efficient as compared to individual isolates and record the maximum adsorption of the heavy metals.

Mythili and Karthikeyan (2011) noted that at pH 5 *Bacillus* sp. and *Staphylococcus* sp. showed the (168.9/157.3 mg/L) biosorption activity. Whereas, at pH 6 the results noted was (182.0/160.4 mg/L), followed by pH 7 (194.5/172.2 mg/L) and at pH 8 (169.7/172.3 mg/L). Similarly at temperature 25°C, the biosorption level noted was (154.6/161.2 mg/L) at 30°C (170.5/168.4 mg/L), 35°C (192.4/172.6 mg/L) and 40°C (176.1/169.7 mg/L). The results showed that pH 7 and temperature 35°C were found to be optimum for both *Bacillus* sp. and *Staphylococcus* sp. for the biosorption study From the optimization study, the effective pH 7 and temperature 35°C was maintained in tannery effluent for *Bacillus* sp. and *Staphylococcus* sp. The efficiency of the results noted was 86 and 74 per cent respectively.

Smrithi and Usha (2012) isolated thirty four bacterial strains which belongs to different bacterial genera, the dominant being *Bacillus, Micrococcus* and *Lactobacillus* sp. The most suitable temperature for chromium (Cr) resistant bacterial isolate was found to be 37°C. Bacterial Cr(VI) reduction was found to be maximum at 25°C to 30°C for five bacterial isolates and higher temperature (above 37°C) severely retarded Cr(VI) bioreduction. The optimum pH for the growth of Cr resistant bacteria was reported as pH 7 to 7.8. But, Cr forms are soluble over a wide range of pH and generally mobile in soil - water systems. The optimum initial pH was 7.0 to 9.0 which corresponded to a final pH of 6.8 to 6.2. Similar findings were noticed by Vainshtein *et al.* (2003), Faryal *et al.* (2007) and Benedict *et al.* (2008).

Srinivasu *et al.* (1999) reported that the pH and temperature changed during the bioremediation process due to metabolic activities. Vidali (2001) suggested that the microbial growth and activity are readily affected by pH, temperature and moisture. However, although microorganisms have also been isolated in extreme conditions, most of them grow optimally over a narrow range

It was demonstrated that the maximum adsorption of heavy metal was achieved by immobilized consortia at temperature 28°C, 5 per cent inoculum load and when ammonium nitrate and sucrose were used as nitrogen and carbon source at 30 hrs incubation. Similar results were reported by Frankenberger *et al.* (2003) who reported that the maximum adsorption at 28°C temperature were noticed. Pillar Pons and Fuste (1993) reported that maximum adsorption occurs at high inoculum load. This result indicates a 'screen effect' among the dense layer of cells, leading to 'protection of the binding sited from metal ions'. In other words, the metal uptake is higher when the intercellular distance was more, as this condition ensures optimal electrostatic interaction between cells with a significant factor of biosorption. Monda *et al.* (2008) suggested that cell age was considered as an important microbial factor that affects metal accumulation.

Lowest metal removal by all the strains were observed with 0.5 per cent inoculum volume as where highest Cr(VI), Ni(II) and Zn(II) degradation was observed at 2.0 per cent inoculum volume. At 2.0 per cent inoculum volume no significant variation in cell growth were observed. This may be due to over populated culture and fixed amount of nutrient with which the organism starts liberating proteolytic enzyme, enhancing self consumption reported by Sankar *et al.* (1998).

5.5. BIOREMEDIATION OF TANNERY EFFLUENT BY IMMOBILIZED BACTERIAL CONSORTIUM

Chromium is the most toxic and common among the heavy metal pollutants of industrial effluents. In this work the chromium remediation ability of *Bacillus subtilis*, *Pseudomonas aeruginosa* and *Saccharomyces cerevisiae* in consortia and in their immobilized forms was studied and their efficiencies were compared. Flame Atomic Absorption Spectroscopy and diphenyl carbazide method was used to quantify chromium in the effluent. The chromium content of the effluent was around 770 mg/L before remediation, after which it reduced to 5.2 – 5.7 mg/L. The best activity was observed by *Saccharomyces cerevisiae - Pseudomonas aeruginosa* consortia followed by immobilized beads of *Saccharomyces cerevisiae* and *Saccharomyces cerevisiae - Bacillus subtilis* consortia (Fathima Benazir *et al.*, 2010).

Filali *et al.* (2000) also reported waste water bacterial isolates *Pseudomonas aeruginosa, Klebsiella pneumoniae, Proteus vulgaris* and *Staphylococcus* sp. resistant to heavy metals (Clausen, 2000). Similarly, Sharma *et al.* (2004) isolated cadmium resistant *Klebsiella* that was found to precipitate significant amount of cadmium.

Sivaruban *et al.*, (2014) studied the remediation ability of *Bacillus subtilis, Pseudomonas aeruginosa* and *Saccharomyces cerevisiae* in consortia and in their immobilized forms for the treatment of tannery effluents. The efficiencies of the microbes were compared towards the improvement of physic-chemical parameters as well as for Chromium (VI) remediation capacity. It was noted that all the three species were tolerant of high dosage of Cr(VI) and have been successful in remedying the Cr(VI). However, immobilization of the species has shown the greatest potential in treating the Cr(VI) containing wastewaters.

In the present study, physico - chemical parameters of the immobilized bacterial consortium (*Bacillus subtilis + Serratia marcescens + Pseudomonas fluorescens*) bioremediated effluent was estimated at sixth month. After treatment with microbial isolates, the effluent turned colourless and odourless, which might be due to the action of microbial isolates. This result was supported by Noorjahan (2005) studied that the tannery effluent was remediated with microorganism after remediation the effluent pH was neutral, EC of effluent 4350µmhos/cm and TSS 32mg/l± 1.8708, TDS 2045mg/L ±1.5811, BOD 36mg/L ±1.5811, COD 297mg/ L ±1.581, Chromium 0.829 mg/ L, and Copper 0.00296 mg/ L.

The TSS and TDS present in bioremediated tannery effluent was 95 mg/L and 108mg/ in the sixth month respectively. The TDS were found to be 108 mg/L in the sixth month. The BOD and COD varied within a span of six months to 220 mg/L and 26 mg/L respectively.

Srinivas Gidhamaari *et al.* (2012) studied the efficiency of immobilized bacteria in tannery effluent treatment. In order to study the bacterial diversity in effluent and treatment of effluent by using immobilized bacteria, the effluent sample was collected from tannery industry. From this, totally 6 species of bacteria such as *Pseudomonas putida, Pseudomonas fluorescens, Klebsiella pneumoniae, Escherichia coli, Staphylococcus aureus* and *Bacillus subtilis* were isolated. Among the genus, *Pseudomonas* was found dominant group of bacteria. A great deal of effort has been made during the last three decade to establish the methods to eliminate the N_2 present in the waste water. The present investigation was carried out by using immobilized bacteria to remove the pollutants from tannery waste water. Really a great result was come out from this studies. Nearly, 50 per cent successful removal of nitrogen components was observed, chloride was difficult to remove by conventional biological treatment, in the present investigation total 24 per cent removal was observed. Due to the immobilized bacteria the BOD and COD level was reduced nearly 75 per cent and 65 per cent respectively. From the present investigation, it was observed that the immobilized bacteria could be used to treat the various industrial effluents.

In the present study, the physico - chemical analysis of tannery effluent revealed that it contained a high amount of pH, electrical conductivity, nitrogen, phosphorus, potassium, copper, zinc, iron, lead and manganese. At the same time when bacterial isolates were applied as consortia in the form of immobilized beads, a substantial reduction was observed in the toxicity of metals as observed by (Wani *et al.*, 2008). The similar results were reported by Glick (2003); Maliwal *et al.* 2004); Zhuang *et al.* (2007) and Baskaran *et al.* (2009).

6. SUMMARY

- The tannery effluent was collected from the Vellore district of Tamil Nadu, India and bioremediated.

- Physico – chemical characteristics of the collected tannery effluent was analyzed. The tannery effluent was acidic nature with brown colour and emitted unpleasant smell. High value of TSS and TDS and BOD and COD, calcium, magnesium, sodium, potassium, fluoride, nitrate, nitrite, sulphate and the toxic heavy metals chromium, nickel, zinc, copper and iron were recorded in the collected tannery effluent sample.

- The number of microbial isolates present in the collected tannery effluent was enumerated by spread plate technique. In the tannery effluent, the population of bacterial isolates was very high followed by fungal and actinomycetes isolates.

- Ten different bacterial isolates *viz.*, *Pseudomonas* sp. (P1), *Proteus* sp., *Bacillus* sp., *Escherichia* sp., *Serratia* sp., *Pseudomonas* sp. (P2), *Staphylococcus* sp., *Enterobacter* sp., *Alcaligenes* sp., *Micrococcus* sp. and *Staphylococcus* sp. were identified.

- The bacterial isolates were screened for its resistance against toxic heavy metals. All the ten isolate were resistant to all the heavy metals.

- Heavy metal adsorption by living bacterial cells (Bioaccumulation), dead bacterial cells (Biosorption) and immobilized bacterial cells (Immobilization) was studied. Immobilized (Sodium alginate) bacterial cells were considered as the best was for the bioremediation of heavy metals.

- The bacterial isolates which were identified in genus level were subjected to 16S rRNA sequencing and identified in species level. The bacteria *Bacillus* sp. confirmed as was confirmed as *Bacillus subtilis*, *Serratia* sp. was confirmed as *Serratia marcescens* and *Pseudomonas* sp. was confirmed as *Pseudomonas fluorescens*.

- The bacterial isolate *Bacillus subtilis*, *Serratia marcescens*, *Pseudomonas fluorescens* were selected for optimization study based on heavy metal adsorption.

➢ The effect of pH (6, 7 and 8), temperature (25°C, 30°C and 40°C), carbon sources (glucose, sucrose, maltose and dextrose), nitrogen sources (peptone, yeast extract, ammonium chloride and ammonium nitrate), biomass concentration (2%, 3%, 4% and 5%) and incubation hours (12 hrs, 18 hrs, 24 hrs and 30 hrs) on heavy metals adsorption by the immobilized bacterial strains were investigated.

➢ It was concluded that pH 7, temperature of 30°C, dextrose as the carbon source, ammonium nitrate as nitrogen source, 5 per cent inoculum load and 30 hrs of incubation time were found as optimum for the treatment with bacterial consortium to be more efficient as compared to individual isolates and record the maximum adsorption of the heavy metals.

➢ The viability of bacteria isolates in alginate beads was observed upto six months. The population of the microbes was increased in both consortium and single inoculants packets during the first month of storage and thereafter reduced with increases in the period of storage upto six months.

➢ The collected tannery effluent was inoculated with (immobilized beads) 5 per cent inoculum containing $>10^5$ cfu/ml of bacterial consortium (*Bacillus subtilis* + *Serratia marcescens* + *Pseudomonas fluorescens*), and air was passed continuously using an aerator. After 6 months, the sample was filtered under aseptic condition and physico - chemical parameters were estimated.

➢ The colour of the bioremediated tannery effluent sample was black to colourless and odorless. The physico – chemical characteristics of the bioremediated tannery effluent was significantly reduced after 6 months.

7. CONCLUSION

The present study, concludes that the physico - chemical parameters and heavy metals contents were very high in effluents released by tannery industries. The tannery effluents were accumulated in soil, water bodies and it's toxic to plants, animals and humans. The immobilized bacterial consortium (*Bacillus subtilis* + *Serratia marcescens*+ *Pseudomonas fluorescens*) were used for the bioremediated the tannery effluent. The physico-chemical parameters are gradually reduced after the six month of the treatment. Remediation with microorganisms is an easy, effective, economical and eco-friendly. The treated effluents with immobilized bacterial consortium are not offensive and they satisfy the ISI standard values and therefore can be used for irrigation purpose.

8. REFERENCES

1) Abou Shanab, R.A., K. Ghanem, N. Ghanem, A. Al-Kolaibe. 2008. The role of bacteria on heavy metal extraction and uptake by plants growing on multi-metal contaminated soils. *World Journal of Microbiology and Biotechnology*, 24(2): 253 - 262.

2) Acevedo-Aguilar, F.J., A.E. Espino-Saldan, I.L. Leon-Rodriguez. 2006. Hexavalent chromium removal in vitro and from industrial wastes, using chromate-resistant strains of filamentous fungi indigenous to contaminated wastes. *Can J of Microbiol*, 52: 809 - 815.

3) Aksu, Z. and S.S. Çagatay. 2006. Investigation of biosorption of Gemazol Turquise Blue-G reactive dye by dried *Rhizopus arrhizus* in batch and continuous systems. *Sep. Purif. Technol.*, 48: 24 - 35.

4) Alam , M.Z ., S. Ahmad and A. Malik. 2009. Genotoxic and mutagenic potential of agricultural soil irrigated with tannery effluents at Jaimau (Kanpur), India Arch. *Environ. Contant .Toxicol.*, 57: 463 - 476.

5) Al-Enezi,F. 2005. Academic Achievement and its Relationship with Anxiety, Self- Esteem, Optimism and Pessimism in Kuwaiti Students. *Social Behaviour and Personality,* 33(1): 95-104.

6) Altaf, M.M., F. Masood and A. Malik. 2008. Impact of long term application of treated tannery effluent on the emergence of resistance traits in *Rhizobium* sp. Isolated from *Trifolium alexandrium*. *Turkey Journal of Biology*, 32:1 - 8.

7) Alvarez-Bernal, D., S.M. Contreras-Ramos, N. Trujillo-Tapia, V. Olalde-Portugal, J.T. Frias-Hernandez and L. Dendooven. 2006. Effects of tanneries wastewater on chemical and biological soil characteristics. *Appl. Soil Ecol.*, 33: 269 - 277.

8) Amalesh Samanta, Paramita Bera, Mahamuda Khatun, Chandrima Sinha, Pinaki Pal, Asif Lalee and Anurup Mandal. 2012. An investigation on heavy metal tolerance and antibiotic resistance properties of bacterial strain *Bacillus*

sp. isolated from municipal waste. *Journal of Microbiology and Biotechnology Research*, 2(1): 178 - 189.

9) Amathussalam, A., M.N. Abusbacker and N.J. Jayabal. 2002. Physico-chemical parameters and concentration of heavy metals in sugar industry. *Indian Pollution Control*, 13: 118 - 119.

10) American Public Health Association (APHA) 2005. Standard methods for the examination of water and waste water, 21st edition, American water works association, Water Environment federation, Washington DC.

11) Aneez Mohamed, M., P. Sekar and George John. 2011. Efficacy of Microbes in Bioremediation of Tannery Effluent. *International Journal of Current Research.,* 33(4): 324 - 326.

12) Angela, R., Bielefeldt and Catherine.2014. Stability of biologically reduced chromium in soil. *Journal of Environmental Chemical Engineering*, 2: 550 - 556.

13) Anne Spain and Elizabeth Alm. 2003. Implications of Microbial Heavy Metal Tolerance in the Environment. *Reviews in Undergraduate Research*, 2: 1 - 6.

14) Anon. 1992. Standard methods of water and waste water examination. 18th Edition. American Public Health Association, Washington, DC. 37: 2 - 12.

15) AOAC. 2005. Official Method of Analysis 14th edition. AOAC, Inc. Arlington.

16) Azza, O. F., E. Afaf and M. Galal. 2009. Toxicopathological effects of *Guiera senegalensis* extracts in wistar albino rats. *J. Med. Plants Res.* 3(10): 699 – 702.

17) Babich, H., M. Schiffen Bauer and G. Statzky . 1892. Effect of sterilization method on toxicity of Cr 3+ and Cr 6+ to fungi. *Microbios letters*, 20 (78): 55 - 64.

18) Barajas-Aceves, M., R. Velasquez-Ocampo and R. Vazquez-Rodriguez. 2007. Effects of Cr3+, Cr6+ and tannery sludge on C and N mineralization and microbial activity in semi-arid soils. *J. Hazard. Mater.*, 143: 522 - 531.

19) Barman, S.C., S.K. Sahu, S.K. Bhargava and C. Chatterjee, 2000. Distribution of heavy metals in Wheat, mustard and grown in field irrigated with industrial effluent. *Bulletin of Environmental and Contamination Toxicology*, 64: 489 - 496.

20) Baskaran, L., K. Sankar Ganesh, A. L. A. Chidambaram and P. Sundaramorthy. 2009. Amelioration of sugar mill effluent polluted soil and its effect of green gram. *Botany Research International,* 2 (2): 131- 135.

21) Belay, A.A. 2010. Impacts of chromium from tannery effluent and evaluation of alternative treatment options. *Journal of Environmental Protection*, 1: 53-58.

22) Benedict, C., L. Okeke, J. Laymon and Crenshaw SOJIC. 2008. Environmental and kinetic parameters for Cr (VI) bioreduction by a bacterial monoculture purified from Cr (VI) resistant consortium. *Biol. Trace Element Res.*, 123: 229 - 241.

23) Bento, G and K. Okeke. 2003. Chromate reduction by chromium resistant bacteria isolated from soils contaminated with dichromate. *Journal of Environment Quality,* 32: 1228 - 1233.

24) Bhalli, J.A. and M.K. Quiser. 2006. Pollution level analysis in tannery effluents collected from three different cities of Punjab. *Pak.J.Biol.Sci.*, 9 (3): 418-421.

25) Carmen Fuste, M. and Pillai pons .1993. Uranium uptake by immobilized cells of *Pseudomonas* strain EPS 5028. *Applied microbiology and biotechnology,* 39: 661-665.

26) Cervantes, C., F.B. Holl, N.A. Cardova and De Na Mora. 1986. Resistance to metal by *Pseudomonas aeruginosa.* Clinical Isolates Microbiol. 4: 159-163.

27) Chandra, P. and K. Kulsheshtha. 2004. Chromium Accumulation and Toxicity in Aquatic Vascular Plants. *Botanical Review*, 70(3): 313 - 327.

28) Cheung, K.H. and D. Gu, Ji. 2007. Mechanism of hexavalent chromium detoxification by microorganisms and bioremediation application potential: A review. Int. *Biodeter. Biodegr.*, 59: 8 - 15.

29) Chunillal, V., A. Kindness and S.B. Jonnaladda. 2005. Heavy metal uptake by two edible Ammaranthus herbs grown on soil contaminated with lead, mercury, cadmium and nickel. *Journal of Environmental Science and Health*, 40: 375 - 384.

30) Clausen, C.A. 2000. Isolating metal-tolerant bacteria capable of removing copper, chromium, and arsenic from treated wood. Waste Manage Res., 18: 264-268.

31) Colak, S., H. M.M. Ozgunay and F. Mutlu, Akyuz. 2005. Reducing the amount of tanning materials passing into wastewater in post- tanning processes. *Journal of American health chemists Association*, 100(3): 111 -119.

32) Congeevaram, S., S. Dhanarani, J. Park, M. Dexilin and K. Thamaraiselvi. 2007. Biosorption of chromium and nickel by heavy metal resistant fungal and bacterial isolates. *J. Hazard. Mater.* 146: 270 - 277.

33) Contreras-Ramos, S.M., D. Alvarez-Bernal, N. Trujillo-Tapia and L. Dendooven. 2004. Composting of tannery effluent with cow manure a wheat straw. *Bioresource Technology*, 94: 223 - 228.

34) Costa, A. C. A., E.S. Cossich and S.G.F. Leite. 2000. Metals biosorption by sodium alginate immobilized *Chlorella homosphaera*. *Biotechnology Letters*, 13: 55 - 56.

35) Crawford, J.H. 1983. Composting of agricultural wastes - a review. *Process Biochemistry,* 18: 14 - 18.

36) Das, S.K. and A.K. Guha. 2007. Biosorption of chromium by Termitomyces clypeatus. *Colloid Surf.*, 60: 46 - 54.

37) De Nicola, E., S. Meric, C. Della rocca, M. Gallo, M. Iacearine, P. Manini, D. Petruzzelli, V. Belgiomo, N. Cheggour, A. Di gennaro, A. Moukrim, O. Tunay and G. Pagano. 2007. Waste water toxicity of tannin- based leather tanneries in Marrakesh, Morocco. *Environmental contamination and Toxicology*, 53: 321 - 328.

38) Devarajan, L., G. Rajannan, G. Ramanathan and G. Oblisami. 1993. Studies on the effect of alcohol distillery effluent on soil fertility status, yield and quality of crop produce, Final report.TNAU, Coimbatore -3. 159

39) Doenmez, G. and Z. Aksu. 2001. Bioaccumulation of copper(II) and Nickel (II) by the non adapted and adapted growing *Candida* sp. *Wat. Res.*, 35: 1425-1434.

40) Ebtesam, E.l., Bestawy ,Shacker Helmy, Hany Hussien and Mohamed Fahmy, Ranya Amer. 2013. Bioremediation of heavy metal-contaminated effluent using optimized activated sludge bacteria. *Appl Water Sci.*, 3: 181 - 192.

41) EPA. 1998. Methods for chemical analysis of industrial effluents. Environmental Protection Agency, USA.

42) Faryal, R., M. Yusuf, K. Munil, F. Tahir and A. Hameed. 2007. Enhancement of Cr6+ removal by *Aspergillus niger* RH1 using a Biofermenter. *Pak. J. Bot.*, 39 (5): 1873 - 1881.

43) Fathima Benazi, J., R. Suganthi, D. Rajvel, M. Padmini Pooja and B. Mathithumilan. 2010. Bioremediation of chromium in tannery effluent by microbial consortia. *African Journal of Biotechnology,* 9 (21):3140-3143.

44) Filali. B.K., J.Taoufik, Y. Zeroual, F.Z. Dzairi, M. Talbi and M. Blaghen. 2000. Waste water bacteria resistant to heavy metals and antibiotics. *Current Microbiology,* 41: 151-156.

45) Franco, A.r., C.S.C. Calheiros, C.C. Pacheco, P. Marco, C.M. Manaia and P.M.L. Castro. 2005. Isolation and characterization of polymeric Galloyl-

Ester- degrading bacteria from a tannery discharge place. *Microbial Ecology*, 50: 550 - 556.

46) Frankenberger ,R., N. Roth S. Kramer N. Pelka M. Petschelt. 2003. Effect of preparation mode on Class II resin composite repair. *J Oral Rehabil.*, 30: 559 - 564.

47) Fukuda, T., Y. Ishino, A. Ogawa, K. Tsutsumi, H. Morita. 2008. Cr(VI) reduction from contaminated soils by *Aspergillus* SP. N2 and *Pencillium* SP. N3 isolated from chromium deposits. *J Gen Appl Microbiol.,* 54: 295 - 303.

48) Fulekar, M.H and J. Sharma. 2008. Bioinformatics applied in bioremediation. *Innovative Romaninan Food Biotechnology*, 2 (2): 28 - 36.

49) Gadd, G.M. 2010. Metals, minerals and microbes: Geomicrobiology and bioremediation. Microbiology. 156: 609 - 643.

50) Giannis ,A., E. Gidarakos and A. Skouta. 2008. Transport of cadmium and assessment of phytotoxicity after electrokinetic remediation. *J Environ Manage*, 86: 535 - 544.

51) Gong, R., X. Zhang, H. Liu, Y. Sun and B. Liu B. 2007. Uptake of cationic dyes from aqueous solution by biosorption onto granular kohlrabi peel. *Biores. Technol.*, 98: 1319 - 1323.

52) Gouda, M.K. 2000. Studies on chromate reduction by three *Aspergillus* species. Fresen. *Environ. Bull.* 9: 799 - 808.

53) Gupta, A.K. and S. Sinha. 2007. Phytoextraction capacity of the *Chenopodium album* L. grown on soil amended with tannery sludge. *Bioresource Technology.*, 98: 442 - 446.

54) Gupta, A.K., M. Yunus and P. Pandey. 2003. Bioremediation in eco-technology for the present century. *Inter. Soc. Environ. Botanists Environnews*, 2: 9-11.

55) Hsua, M.J., B.K. Selvaraj and G. Agoramoorthy. 2006. Taiwan's Industrial Heavy metal pollution threatens terrestrial Biota. *Environmental Pollution*, 143 (2): 327 - 334.

56) Huguet, A., L. Vacher. S. Relexana, S. Saubusse, J.M. Froidefond and E. Parlanti E. 2009. Properties of fluorescent dissolved organic matter in the Gironde Estuary. *In: Organic Geochemistry*, 40: 706 - 719.

57) Hussein,H., H. Moawad and S. Farag. 2004. Isolation and characterization of *Pseudomonas* resistant to heavy metals contaminants. *Arab J. Biotech.,* 7 (1): 13 - 22.

58) Ilhan, S., N.M. Nourbakhsh, S. Kilicarslan and H. Ozdag. 2004. Removal of chromium, lead and copper ions from industrial waste waters by Staphylococcus saprophyticus. *Turkish Electronic Journal of Biotechnology,* 2, 50-57.

59) Jackson, J. 1973. The Remedial options for metal contaminated sites. *Current Opinions in Biotechnology*, 5: 285 - 290.

60) James Bruce, R. 2002. Chemical transformations of chromium in soils. *J. Chem. Environ.,* 6(2): 46 - 48.

61) Jimenez, F.M.G., A.R.N. Munoz, L.M. Barrea and E.C. Urbina. 2009. Hexavalent Chromium removal by *Candida* sp. In a concentric draft tube airlift Bioreactor. *Water Air and Soil pollution,* 204: 43 - 51.

62) Johncy Rani M., P.M. Pons and S. Sumathi. 2010. Uranium uptake by immobilized cells of *Pseudomonas* sp. strains EPS 5028, *Bacillus* sp. and *Micrococcus* sp. *Appl. Microbiol. Biotechnol.,* 39: 661- 665.

63) Kamaludeen, S.P.B., M. Megharaj, R. Naidu, I. Singleton, A.L. Juhasz, B.G. Hawke and N. Sethunathan. 2003. Microbial activity and phospholipid fatty acid pattern in long-term tannery waste-contaminated soil. *Ecotox. Environ. Safe.,* 56: 302 - 310.

64) Kapoor, A. and T. Viraraghavan and D.R. Cullimore. 1999. Removal of heavy metals using the fungus *Aspergillus niger. Bioresource Technology*, 70: 95 - 104.

65) Kapoor, A. and T. Viraraghavan. 1998. Application of immobilized *Aspergillus niger* biomass in the removal of heavy metals from an industrial waste water. *J. Environ. Sci. Hlth.,* 133 (7) : 1507 - 1514.

66) Karami, Ali and J. Shamsuddin Zulkifli. 2010. Phytoremediation of heavy metals with several efficiency enhancer methods. *African journal of biotechnology.* 9(25): 3689-3698.

67) Karthikeyan, K., C. Chandran and S. Kulothangan. 2010. Biodegradation of oil sludge of petroleum waste from automobile service station using selected fungi. *Journal of Ecotoxicology and Environmental Monitoring,* 20(3): 225 - 230.

68) Katiyar, S.K. and R. Katiyar. 1997. Microbes in control of heavy metal pollution. *Adv. Microb. Biotechnol.,* 19: 330-344.

69) Kawser Ahmed, Md., Monika Das, Monirul Islam and Mosammat Salma Akter. 2011. Physico - chemical properties of Tannery and Textile effluents and surface water of river Buriganga and Karnatoli, Bangladesh. *World Applied Sciences Journal,* 12 (2): 152 - 159.

70) Khan, N.A., I. Ahmad, S. Singh and R. Nazar. 2006. Variation in growth, photosynthesis and yield of five wheat cultivars exposed to cadmium stress. *World J. Agric. Sci.,* 2: 223-226.

71) Khilji, S. and F. Barbeen. 2008. Rhizofiltration of heavy metals form the tannery sludge by the anchored hydrophyte, hydrophyte unbellata. *American Journal of Biotechnology,* 7 (20): 3711 - 3717.

72) Kiran. I., T. Akar and S. Tunali. 2005. Biosorption of Pb (II) and Cu (II) from aqueous solution by pretreated biomass of *Neurospora crassa*. Process Biochem., 40: 3550- 3558.

73) Kisku, G.C.S., S.C. Barman and S.K. Bhargava. 2000. Contamination of soil and plants potentially toxic elements irrigated with mixed industrial effluent and impact in the environment. *Journal of Water, Air and Soil Pollution*, 120: 121 - 137.

74) Kumar, K. V., V. Ramamurthi and S. Sivanesan. 2006. Biosorption of malachite green, a cationic dye onto *Pithophora* sp., fresh water algae. *Dyes Pigments*, 69: 102 -107.

75) Kurt, U., O. Apaydin, M.T. Gonullu, J. Hazard. 2007. Effect of alkaline treatments at various temperature on cellulase and biomass producing using submerged sugarcane baggage fermentation with *Trichoderma reesei. Mater.* 2007. 143: 33.

76) Lavanya and Venkatakrishnan. 1997. Bioethics in India: Proceedings of the International Bioethics workshop in Madras. *Biomanagement of Biogeoresources*, 16- 19.

77) Lefebvre, O., Vasudevan, N., Torrijos, M., Thanasekaran, K., Moletta, R. (2006). Anaerobic digestion of tannery soak liquor with an aerobic post-treatment.Water Res.;40:1492–1500.

78) Leusch, A., Z.R. Holan and B.J. Volesky. 2005. Biosorption of heavy metals in water supplies production of oil industry. *Journal of Chemical Technology and Biotechnology*, 62: 279 – 288.

79) Lone, M.I., Z. He, P.J. Stoffella and X. Yang. 2008. Phytoremediation of heavy metals polluted soils and water progress and perspectives. *J. Zhejiang Univ. Sci.* B., 9(3): 210 - 220.

80) Mahavi, R. 2005. Biotechnology applications to environmental remediation in resources exploitation. *Current Science*, 97: 6 - 25.

81) Malik, D.M., M.Z. Khan and T.A. Chaudhary. 1984. Analysis Manual for soils, plants and waters. Punjab, Lahore: Soil fertility Survey and soil testing Institute, Department of Agriculture, p.24.

82) Maliwal, G.L., K.P. Patel, K.C. Patel and M.N. Patel, 2004. Pollution studies on sugar mill effluent, physico-chemical properties and toxic metals. *Pollution Research*, 14: 231-238.

83) Megharaj, M., S. Avudainayagam and R. Naidu. 2003. Toxicity of hexavalent chromium and its reduction by bacteria isolated from soil contaminated with tannery waste. *Current Microbiology*, 47: 51 - 54.

84) Mehdi, S. M., G. Abbas, M. Sarfraz, S.T. Abbas and G. Hassan. 2003. Effect of industrial effluents on mineral nutrition of rice and soil health. *Pakistan Journal Applied Sciences, 3*: 462 - 473.

85) Monda,M., A. Viggiano, A.Viggiano, R. Mondola, E.Viggiano and G. Messina. 2008b.Olanzapineblocksthesympatheticandhyperthermic reactions due to *Cerebralinjectiono forexin* A. *Peptides.,* 29: 120- 126.

86) Morales-Barrera, L. and E. Cristiani-Urbina. 2008. Hexavalent chromium removal by a *Trichoderma inhamatum* fungal strain isolated from tannery effluent. *Water Air Soil Pollut* ., 187: 327 - 336.

87) Mungasavalli, D.P., T. Viraraghavan, C. Jin and Yee. 2007. Biosorption of chromium from aqueous solutions by pretreated *Aspergillus niger*: Batch and column studies. *Colloid Surface A 301*, 214 - 223.

88) Mustafa, S., T. Ahmad, A. Naum, K.H. Shah and M. Wassum. 2010. Kinetics of chromium ion removal from tannery wastes using Amberliti IRA 400c and its hybrids. *Water, Air and Soil pollution,* 210(1-4): 43 - 50.

89) Mythili, K. and B. Karthikeyan. 2011. Bioremediation of Chromium [Cr (VI)] In Tannery Effluent Using *Bacillu* spp and *Staphylococcus* spp. *International Journal of Pharmaceutical & Biological Archives*, 2(5): 1460 - 1463.

90) Mythili, K. and B. Karthikeyan. 2011. Bioremediation of tannery effluent and its impact on seed germination (blackgram and sunflower). *Current Botany*, 2(8): 40 - 45.

91) Nagarajan, P., T.R. Moorthy, R.E. Raja and A.P. Raj. 2005. Physico-chemical characteristics of water and soil at Senthanirpuram, Thiruchirapalli and their influence on germination on green gram and cowpea. *J. Ecotoxicol. Environ. Monitor.*, 15 (3): 229 - 234.

92) Natarajan K.A. 1988. Electrochemical aspects of bioleaching multisulfide minerals. *Minerals metallurg process,* 61-65.

93) Nies , H. 2003. Efflux-mediated heavy metal resistance in prokaryotes Dietrich.. *FEMS Microbiology Reviews*, 27 :319-339.

94) Noorjahan, Sharief and Dawood. 2005.Biodegradation of dairy effluent. *Pollut. Res.*, 24: 101-104.

95) Nouri, J., N. Khorasani, B. Lorestani, M. Karami, A.H. Hassani and N. Yousefi. 2005. Accumulation of heavy metals in soil and uptake by plant species with phytoremediation potential. *Environment and Earth Science*, 59: 315 - 323.

96) Okeyode, C. and I.A. Moshood. 2010. Elemental compositions of the soil of Ogun- osun river basins development authority Headquarters, Ogun- state, Nigeria. *Indian Journal of Science and Technology*, 3(3): 335 - 336.

97) Palaniappan, P.L.R.M., N. Krishnakumar and M. Vadivelu. 2009. Bioaccumulation of lead and the influence of chelating agents in *Catla catla* fingerlings. *Environ Chem Lett.*, 7: 51 - 54.

98) Pandey, G. N. 1997. Environmental Management, Vikas Publishing House Pvt. Ltd., New Delhi. p. 399.

99) Pandey, S.N., B.D. Nautiyal and C.P. Sharma. 2008. Pollution level in distillery effluent and its phytotoxic effect on seed germination and early growth of maize and rice. *Journal of Environmental Biology*, 29(2): 267 - 270.

100) Pankaj Trivedi and Anita Pandey. 2007. Performance of different carrier materials. Biofertilizers Newsletter. 4(2): 7-9.

101) Park, D., Y.S. Yun and J.M. Park. 2005. Use of dead fungal biomass for the detoxification of hexavalent chromium: screening and kinetics. *Process Biochem* ., 40: 2559 - 2565.

102) Pillichshammer, M., T. Pumple, K. Eller, J. Klima and F. Schinner. 1995. Biosorption of chromium to fungi. *Biometals,* 8: 117 - 121.

103) Poornima, M., R. Senthil Kumar and P. Danial Thomas.2014. Isolation and molecular characterization of bacterial Strains from tannery effluent and reduction of chromium *Int.J.Curr.Microbiol.App.Sci.,* 3(4): 530 - 538.

104) Pragati saini and Ajay kumar. 2012. Alleopathic effect of untreated and bacterial treated sewage water on the seedling growth *Zea mays. Asian.Exp.Biol.Sci.,* 3(3): 602 - 606.

105) Preethi,V., K.S.P. Kalyani, C. Srinivasakannan, N. Balasubramaniam, K. Ilyappan and N. Vedaraman, J. 2009. Hazard Mater. *J.Hazard Mater.,* 143: 33.

106) Priya Pillai, G. and A. Archana. 2012. Novel process for biodegradation and effective utilization of chrome shavings, a solid waste generated in tanneries, using chromium resistant *Bacillus subtilis* P13. *Process Biochemistry,* 47: 2116 - 2122.

107) Rahman K.S.M, I.M. Banat, T.J. Rahman, T. Thayumanavan and P. Lakshmanaperumalsamy. 2002. Bioremediation of gasoline contaminated soil by a bacterial consortium amended with poultty litter, coir pith and rhamnolipid biosurfactant. *Bioresour Technol,* 81: 25 - 32.

108) Ravibabu , M.V., C.H. Nagaveni and K. Jamil. 2007. Toxic effect of Industrial effluents on rat: Analysis and remediation methods. *Intern. J. Toxicol.,* 3 (2): 51 - 60.

109) Richard, L.A. 1954. Diagnosis and improvement of saline and alkali soils. Agriculture Hand Book, USDA, p 60.

110) Sadeeshkumar, R., P. Saranraj and D. Annadurai. 2012. Bioadsorption of the toxic heavy metal chromium by using *Pseudomonas putida*. *International Journal of Research in Pure and Applied Microbiology*, 2(4): 32 - 36.

111) Sahasranaman, A. and J. Buljan. 2000. Environment management in Indian tanneries in 34th, LERIQ: 27 - 30.

112) Sahu, S.K., P. Meshram, B.D.Pandey, V.Kumar and T.R. Mankhand. 2007. Removal of chromium(III) by cation exchange resin, Indion 790 for tannery waste treatment. *Hydrometallurgy,* 99: 170-174

113) Sangeetha, R., B. Kamalahasan and N. Karthi. 2012. Use of tannery effluent for irrigation: an evaluative study on the response of antioxidant defenses in maize *(Zea mays)*. *International Food Research Journal*, 19(2): 607 - 610.

114) Sankar, K.M., C.V. Mohan and M.C .Nandeesha.1998. Promotion of substrate based microbial biofilms in ponds – a low cost technology to boost fish production. *NAGA–ICLARM Quarterly,* 21:18 - 22.

115) Saranraj, P., D. Stella and D. Reetha. 2012. Microbial cellulases and its applictions: a review. *International Journal of Biochemistry & Biotech Science*, 1: 1-12.

116) Saranraj, P., V. Sumathi, D. Reetha, and D.Stella. 2010. Decolourization and degradation of Direct azo dyes and Biodegradation of textile dye effluent by using bacteria isolated from textile dye effluent. *J. Ecobiotechnol.* 2(7): 7–11.

117) Say,R., N. Yilmaz and A. Denizli. 2004. Removal of chromium (VI) ions from ssynthesis solutions by the fungus *Penicillum purpurogenum. Eng.Life sci.*, 4: 276 - 280.

118) Schrank .S.G., H.J. Jose, R.F.P.M. Moreira and H.F. Schroder. 2005. Biosorption of iron from Aqueous solution by dried biomass of activated sludge.*Chemosphere,* 60: 644.

119) Seema Sharma and Alok Adholeya. Hexavalent chromium reduction in tannery effluent by bacterial species isolated from tannery effluent contaminated soil. 2012. *Journal of environmental science and technology*, 5 (3): 142 - 154.

120) Selivanovskaya, S.Y. and V.Z. Latypova. 2006. Effects of composted sewage sludge on microbial biomass, activity and pine seedlings in nursery forest. *Waste Manage*, 26: 1253 - 1258.

121) Semra Ihan, Macit Nurbas Nour Baksh, Serpil Kilicarslan and Hurseyin Ozdaj. 2004. Removal of chromium, lead and copper ions from industrial waste waters by *Staphylococcus saprophyticus. Turkish Electronic Journal of Biotechnology*, 2: 50 - 57.

122) Vereheijen G.V. Reddy, R. Banerjee, P. Ravindra Babu and I.L. Kothari. 1996. Microbial degradation of banana waste under solid state bioprocessing using two lingo cellulolytic fungi (*Phylosticia* spp. MPS-001 and *Aspergillus* spp. MPS-002). *Process Biochemistry*, 40: 445 - 451.

123) Shaili Srivastava and Indu Shekhar Thakur. 2006. Evaluation of bioremediation and detoxification potentiality of *Aspergillus niger* for removal of hexavalent chromium in soil microcosm. *Soil Biology and Biochemistry*, 38 (7): 1904 - 1911.

124) Shanker, A.K., V. Ravichandran and G. Pathmanabhan. 2005. Phytoaccumulation of chromium by some multi purpose tree seedlings. *Agrofor Syst.*, 64: 83 - 87.

125) Sharma, S. and A. Adholeya . 2011b. Phytoremediation of Cr contaminated soil using *Aloe vera* and *Chrysopogon zizanioides* along with AM fungi and filamentous saprobe fungi: a research study towards possible practical application. *Mycorrhiza News*, 22(4): 16 - 20.

126) Sharma, S. and A. Adholeya. 2011. Detoxification and accumulation of chromium from tannery effluent and spent chrome effluent by *Paecilomyces lilacinus* fungi. *International Biodeterioration and Biodegradation*, 65: 309 - 317.

127) Sharma, S., S. Kaul, A. Metwally, K.C. Goyal and K.J. Dietz. 2004. Cadmium toxicity to barley (*Hordum vulgare*) as affected by varying Fe nutritional status. *Plant Science*, 166: 1287 - 1295.

128) Shitole, V.H. and S.S. Panvalkar. 2011. Bioremediation of tannery effluent. *J Emp Bio Vol .,* 1(2): 10 -23.

129) Shrey Kankaria, Anusha Andukuri, C.G. Hemamailini, M. Krishnaveni. 2011. Impact of tannery effluent on groundwater and agriculture with a remedial measure a case study. International Conference on Chemical, Biological and Environment Sciences (ICCEBS'2011) Bangkok Dec.

130) Shukla,O.P., U. N. Rai, N. K. Singh, Smita Dubey and V. S. Baghel. 2007. Isolation and characterization of chromate resistant bacteria from tannery effluent. *Journal of Environmental Biology* , 28(2): 399 - 403.

131) Singh and Bhatt. 2005. Growth of *Delbergia sisso* in desert region of western India using municipal effluent and subsequent changes in soil plant chemistry. *Bioresource Technology*, 96: 1019 - 1028.

132) Singh, D.K., D. Kumar and V.P. Singh. 2005. Phytoremediation of contaminated soil. *Journal of Environmental Biology*, 5: 15 - 91.

133) Sivaruban, T., S. Barathy, S. Sivakumar, Mukesh Goel, Ashutosh Das, K. Ravi Kumar and S. Maran. 2014. Microbial Removal of High Concentration Heavy Metal in Tannery. *Resesarch Journal of Pharmaceutical Biological and Chemical Sciences*, 5(4): 217-220.

134) Smrithi, A. and K. Usha. 2012. Isolation and characterization of chromium removing bacteria from tannery effluent disposal site. *International Journal of Advanced Biotechnology and Research*, 3 (3): 644 - 652.

135) Soyaslan, I. and R. Karaguazel. 2007. Investigation of water pollution in the yalvac basin into egirdir lake, Turkey. *Environmental Geology*, 55: 1263 - 1268.

136) Srinivas Gidhamaari, Boominathan and Estari Mamidala. 2012. Studies Of Efficiency Of Immobilized bacteria In Tannery Effluent Treatment. *J.Bio.*Innov., 2(2): 33 - 42.

137) Srinivasu,Boominathan and M.L. De Costa. 1999. Effects of detergents on chlorophyll and starch content of *Brassica juncea* L. *Indian Journal of Botanical Society*, (8): 80 - 81.

138) Sudha, B.R and E. Abraham. 2003. Studies on Cr (VI) adsorption - desorption using immobilized fungal biomass. *Bioresource Technology*, 87: 17- 26.

139) Sundar, K., R. Vidya, A. Mukherjee, M. Chandrasekara. 2010. High Chromium Tolerant Bacterial Strain from River Basin, Impact of tannery pollution. *Research Journal of Environmental and Earth Sciences*, 2(2): 112 - 117.

140) Tesena, J.K. and A.R. Bielefeld. 2002. Low temperature chromium (VI) biotransformation in soil with varying electron acceptor, *J. Environ. Qual.*, 31: 1831 - 1834.

141) Thirunavukarasu, K. and A.C. Lourdraj. 2005. Soil Nutrient availability as influenced by tannery effluent irrigation and amendments application in Sunflower (*Helianthus annus*). *Indian Journal of Ecology,* 32 (1): 29-31.

142) Tmoney, J. F., J. Port, J. Giles, J. Spanier. 1987. Heavy metal and antibiotic resistance in the bacterial flora of sediments of New York Bight. *Appl. Environ. Microbiol.,* 36: 465-472.

143) Tobin ,J. M . and J.C. Roux. 1998. Mucor biosorbent for chromium removal from tannery effluent. *WaleI Res*, 32: 1407.

144) Trasar-Cepeda, C., M.C. Leiros, S. Seoane, F. Gil-Sotres. 2000. Limitations of soil enzymes as indicators of soil pollution. *Soil Biol. Biochem.*, 32: 1867 - 1875.

145) Upreti, R.K., R. Srivastava and U.C. Chaturavedi. 2004. Gut Microflora and toxic metals Chromium as a model. *Indian Journal of Medical Research*, 119: 49 - 59.

146) Vainshtein, M.P., J. Kurchk, A. Mathusch, Vatsourina and A. Wiesner. 2003. Model experiment on the microbial removal of chromium from contaminated ground water. *Water Res.,* 37: 1401 - 1405.

147) Varenyam Achal, Deepika Kumari and Xiangliang Pan. 2011. Bioremediation of Chromium Contaminated Soil by a Brown-rot Fungus, *Gloeophyllum sepiarium. Research Journal of Microbiology*, 6 (2): 166 - 171.

148) Vargas, E., B. Volesky, I. Kiran and T. Akar. 2009. Biosorption of heavy metals in water supplies production of oil industry. J. Chem. Technol. Biotechnol., 62: 279- 288.

149) Vatsouria, A., M. Vainshtein , P.Kuschk, A. Wiessner, D. Kosolapov and M. Kaestner. 2005. Anaerobic co-reduction of chromate and nitrate by bacterial cultures of Staphylococcus epidermidis L-02. *J Ind Microbiol Biotechnol* ., 32: 409 -414.

150) Vidali, M. 2001. Bioremediation: An overview. *Pure Applied Chemistry*, 73: 1163 - 1172.

151) Vijayaraghavan, K and Y. Yeoung Sang. 2007. Chemical modification and Immobilization of *Corynebacterium glutamicum* for biosorption of reactive black 5 from aqueous solution. *Chemical Research*, 46: 608 - 617.

152) Viti, C., A. Pace and L. Giovannetti. 2003. Characterization of chromium resistant bacteria isolated from chromium- contaminated soil by tannery activity. *Current Microbiology*, 46: 1 - 5.

153) Wani, M., T.K. Kirk and R.L. Farrell. 2008. Bioremediation of effluent using Microbial consortia in immobilized beads. *Col. Environ Cons.*, 1(3): 34-36.

154) Waziri, M. 2006. Physicochemical and Bacteriological investigation of surface and ground water of Kumadugu- Yobe Basin, PhD thesis, University of Maiduguri, Nigeria, 88- 96.

155) Wei- Bin, L., S. Jun- Ji, W. Ching- Hsiung and C. Jo - Shu. 2006. Biosorption of lead, copper and cadmium by an indigenous isolate of *Enterobacter* sp. possessing high heavy metal resistance. *Journal of Hazardous Materials*, 134: 80 - 86.

156) Widdel, F., A. Boetius and R.Rabus. 2006. Anaerobic biodegradation of hydrocarbons including methane. In: Dworkin M., Falkow S., Rosenberg E., Schleifer K.-H., Stackebrandt E., editors. *Springer-Verlag.*, 1028–1049.

157) Williams, K. H., P.E. Long, J.A. Davis, Wilkins, N. Guessan, A. L., Steefel, C. I., Yang, Newcomer, Spane, L.J. Kerkhof, McGuinness and Dayvaultand Lovley. 2011. Acetate Availability and its Influence on Sustainable Bioremediation of Uranium-Contaminated Groundwater, *Geomicrobiol. J.,* 28: 519 – 539.

158) Xi, X.Z., T.J. Xin, L.X. Duan, J.Pei. 2009. Isolation, identification and characterization of cadmium resistant *Pseudomonas aeruginosa* strain. *Journal of Central South University Technology,* 16: 0416 - 0421.

159) Yu, X. Z. and J.D. Gu. 2007. Accumulation and distribution of trivalent chromium and effects on hybrid willow (*Salix matsudana, Koidzx alba* L.) metabolism. *Arch Environ Contam Toxicol* , 52: 503 - 511.

160) Zhang, M., Z. Chen, Q. Chen, H. Zou, J. Lou and J. He. 2008. Investigating DNA damage in tannery workers occupationally exposed to trivalent chromium using comet assay. *Mutation Research*, 654(1): 45 - 51.

161) Zhuang, A.H., L. Devarajan and S.J Areivals. 2007. Bioearth composting: A technology for recycling of sugar factory and distillery industry wastes. Environmental Impact Access Monitoring and Management, 16(11): 65-67.